JANE COCHRANE

Walking
in the Footsteps
of Odysseus

A Practical Guide to the
Homeric Paths of Ithaca

A CIP catalogue record for this book is available from the British Library

ISBN 978-1-9162923-5-2

Cover painting and illustrations by Jane Cochrane

Typeset by Loco Design

Cover painting 'Rosy-fingered dawn'
© Jane Cochrane

Jane Cochrane trained as an architect at the Architectural Association in London. As an architect she worked principally on existing buildings, at a housing association and as a conservation architect. For several years she taught at the Bower Ashton School of Art in Bristol. She writes, paints, draws and sometimes makes pots as well. Together with her Greek-speaking husband, Alec Kazantzis, she repaired an old house on the island of Ithaca. She has been visiting since 1982 and has written a book, *Odysseus' Island*, about her time there.

Contents

Introduction

Concept

This book was conceived as a compact walking guide to Ithaca leading the visitor over the ancient footpaths that Homerists, philologists, archaeologists and local people have traditionally identified with the descriptions made by Homer in his epic poem *The Odyssey*.

Paths in Ithaca

Some of the paths described are remote. In particular you may find some paths unclearly marked or temporarily blocked. Walking times given exclude stops for rest or sightseeing. Please be aware that you are ultimately responsible for judging your own capabilities in the light of the conditions you find.

Maps

It is always advisable to use the best map you can find, but with caution. Maps of Ithaca have hugely improved recently, but they are still not perfect. It has been known for maps to show paths that don't exist on the ground, and not to show paths that do exist. In addition goat tracks can easily be mistaken for paths, and paths for goat tracks. Targets and arrows painted on rocks are usually reliable route-markers. The most accurate maps that I have found to date are the Anavasi Topo map of the island (Anavasi Topo Islands Cephalonia - Ithaca Hiking Map 1:65,000/ 1:25,000) plus the Avenza Map (Avenza Systems Inc. Ithaca Trails digital map 'On the Footsteps of Odysseus' made by Paths of Greece/Staridas Geography). The latter can be downloaded onto a smartphone in IOS or Android, it uses 30.5 Mb and costs £6.50 from https://www.avenzamaps.com/maps/854181/ithaca-trails.

INTRODUCTION

Disclaimer

Although the author and walk-checker have done their utmost to ensure the accuracy and currency of all information given in this guide, they cannot accept responsibility for any loss, injury or inconvenience sustained by any person using it.

Landscape and essential background history

The many footpaths crisscrossing the small and mountainous Greek island of Ithaca make it a perfect setting for hikers. All these ancient paths have a fascinating history. Some relate to the 600-year Roman rule of the island, others to the 300-year rule of the Venetians. Some are known only to those who herd sheep or goats along them to this day, as they have from time immemorial. But I will focus on a very specific group of paths – those relating to Homer's story of the island's ancient hero, Odysseus.

Homer's epic poems The Iliad and The Odyssey are among the oldest extant works of Western literature, on which they have had a profound influence. The Iliad tells the story of the ninth year of the Trojan War; The Odyssey tells how King Odysseus, a hero of that war, makes his eventful journey back to his home island of Ithaca. By the time Odysseus arrived back on Ithacan soil, 20 years had passed since he set out to fight in the Trojan War. He left behind his young wife, Penelope, and their baby son, Telemachus. Back in Ithaca, as the years went by, Penelope was besieged by suitors. They assumed that Odysseus was dead, and they wanted to claim his kingdom.

The Trojan War took place towards the end of the Bronze Age around the 13th century BC, but some 500 years passed before Homer wrote about it. During the intervening years a series of natural disasters took place across most of the civilised world. Volcanic eruptions and earthquakes led to the destruction of cities, prolonged periods of drought resulted in crop failure and famine, and these were followed by invasions on land and attack by sea. All but one of the Bronze Age empires collapsed. The Palace Civilisation of the Mycenaean Greeks, the Hittite State in modern Anatolia, the Assyrian Empire of Mesopotamia, the Kassite Kingdom of Babylonia, and the Elamite Empire in the area of modern Iran, were all laid to waste. Only the Egyptian New Kingdom survived, but in a much-weakened state.

The years that followed this collapse are called the Dark Ages. Then, around the 8th century BC, things began to change. A new flexible Greek alphabet was developed and the extraordinary Greek culture and civilisation emerged. Homer was at the vanguard of this movement. Exactly who 'Homer' was, his origins, and whether 'he' was one or several poets, is still debated by scholars. But whoever he was, and wherever he came from, we know that the events of the Trojan War that he described took place some 400 or 500 years before his time, in the final years of the Bronze Age and before the Dark Ages.

Even today the people from the Greek island of Ithaca set out and travel the globe. In this they reflect the story of Odysseus, who based his kingdom there. Like him, wherever they go, they long to return to their stunningly beautiful island in the Ionian Sea on the Adriatic side of mainland Greece. In Homer's Odyssey, 15 of the 24 books (Books 1, 2, and 12–24) are located on Ithaca. Homer describes the features of the landscape of Ithaca carefully and, the extraordinary thing is, they correspond very precisely with the places you can still find there today.

To point to specific connections between the landscape, caves and archaeological sites of Ithaca, and the corresponding passages in The Odyssey, I have quoted the relevant extracts from the Penguin Classics edition translated by E. V. Rieu. I have included book and line references so the reader can look these up in any translation into English they happen to have.

With this guide walkers can visit the places described and judge for themselves how well the present-day sites fit with the descriptions made by Homer over 3,000 years ago.

You should start your journey in the footsteps of Odysseus from Vathi, the current capital of Ithaca in the south of the island. See my Map no.1 Island of Ithaca (page 13) showing the locations of my detailed maps nos. 2-8 (pages 14-20).

Testing the walks

We tested the walks described here using the Anavasi Topo map of the island plus, on a smartphone, the Avenza map, plus a good compass. Often we used all three in conjunction and I do recommend that you do this. You will find a few discrepancies between the two maps but we have tried to give you the information on the ground as of summer 2021. The Topo map is the best printed map of Ithaca currently on sale – please don't be tempted to buy an inferior brand as a faulty map can be extremely dangerous. The Avenza map is beautiful. It is sometimes a bit difficult (but not impossible) for oldies to operate, but we found it very useful. In spite of having all this equipment plus a considerable amount of walking experience in this type of venture, we can testify that it is still possible to get lost.

Getting lost

Please heed the following warning about tackling the high paths of this rocky little island. Ithaca is not a large island but you can still lose your way. I will paint a scenario you may come to recognise:

You start off walking along a clear track, chatting merrily to your companion. The scenery is beautiful and the weather is perfect. You have a bottle of water, a hiking stick, a Topo map, a compass, and the Avenza map on your fully charged smartphone. But, as you walk on, a new thought crosses your mind. You realise a bit of time has passed since you last saw one of those neat little blue and white markers laid down by the Avenza mapping team to mark the trail. Looking around you find you have a choice of paths ahead – but some may just be goat tracks and you don't know which to take. Perhaps some are just pebbly paths left by water run-off during the previous winter. You sit down to assess the situation. You bring up the Avenza map on your phone and a little blue spot marks your position. A dotted line shows the position of the path you were following and a bend in the path where you went astray. The place where you walked straight on, when you should have turned round to the right, is quite a way back now, and you don't want to turn back. You reckon that if you take a shortcut north, you will soon re-join the proper path. So you set off on a clear track heading that way but, after a few minutes, it leads into a thicket of trees. Then a fallen tree is blocking the path, so you scramble around it. Things are getting a bit nasty. The pebbles underfoot are slippery and prickly plants wrap themselves around your bare legs. You try the same routine again. By now there are cuts on your legs and you wish you had worn long trousers instead of shorts. You reach a clearing and, yet again, you sit down on a shady rock while you re-assess. You find that the orange tracking mark on the Avenza map on your phone has formed itself into a solid little blob with the blue positioning spot sitting right in the middle of it. The bad news is that you have been walking to and fro, and round and round, with your pathways forming a complicated knotted pattern. My advice may seem counter-intuitive, but on Ithaca it is best never to take a short-cut! As soon as you find you are off-piste, retrace your steps carefully until you are back on track. Even at this late stage it is the best thing to do. Then, when you are on-piste, follow the markers diligently. An Ithacan shepherd, or those who grew up on the island, know these old tracks with an extraordinary instinct, but for us foreigners it is different and it is best to be a bit humble about this. We need to admit our own vulnerability – even with all our clever first-world equipment.

"And now, to convince you,

let me show you the

Ithacan scene."

The goddess Athena to Odysseus
The Odyssey, Book 13: 344

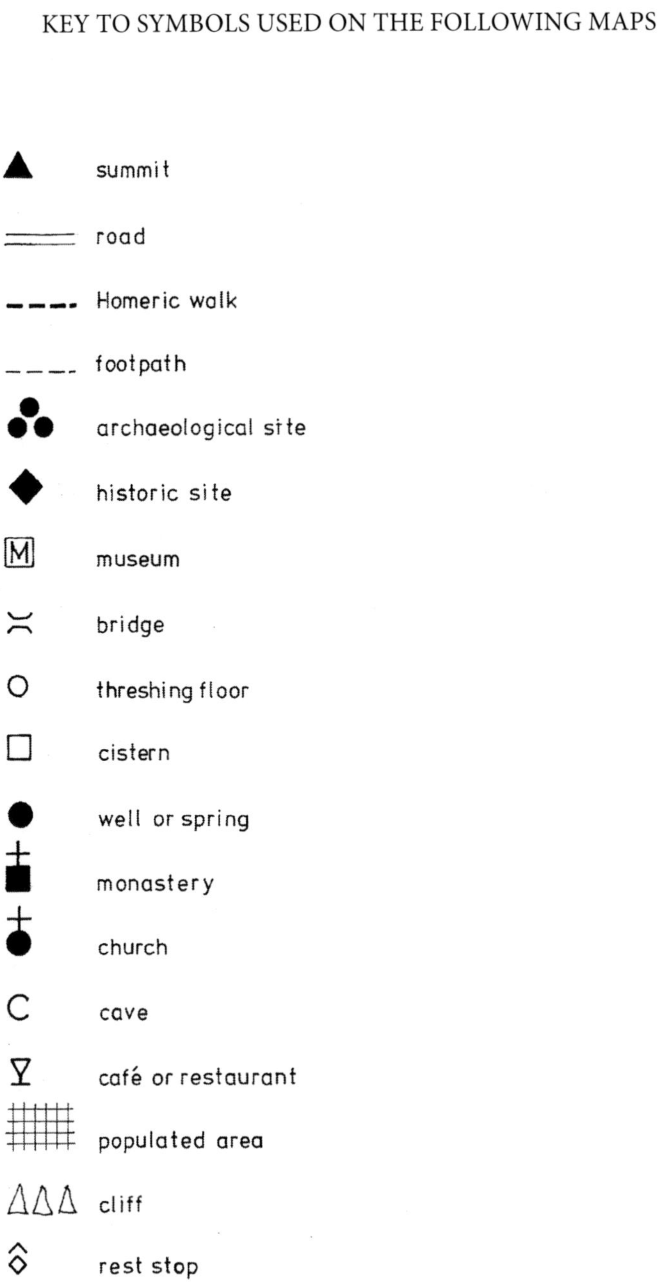

▲ summit

═══ road

━ ━ ━• Homeric walk

_ _ _. footpath

⬤⬤ archaeological site
⬤

◆ historic site

Ⓜ museum

⚊ bridge

○ threshing floor

□ cistern

⬤ well or spring

✝ monastery
■

✝ church
⬤

C cave

Ⴤ café or restaurant

▦ populated area

△△△ cliff

◈ rest stop

Key to symbols used on the following maps

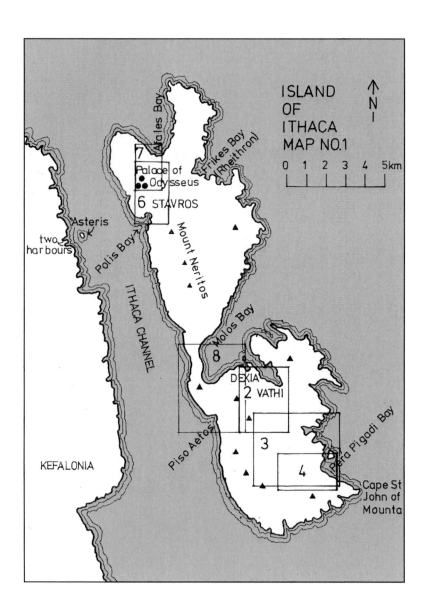

Map no. 1: Island of Ithaca

Numbered rectangles refer to map numbers on the following pages

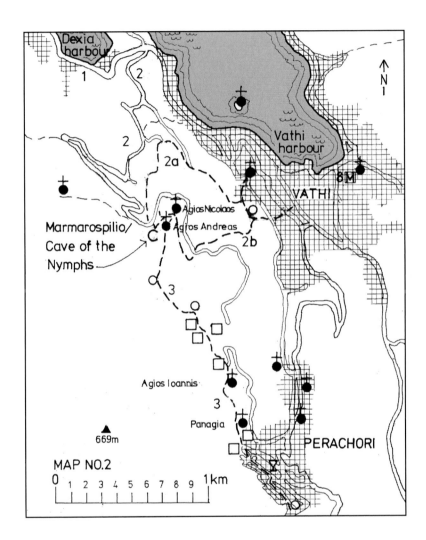

Map no. 2: Odysseus arrives home, leaves his treasure in the cave of the Nymphs and walks on towards Eumaeus' Hut

Numbers adjacent to footpaths on this and the following maps refer to the chapter numbers in this guide

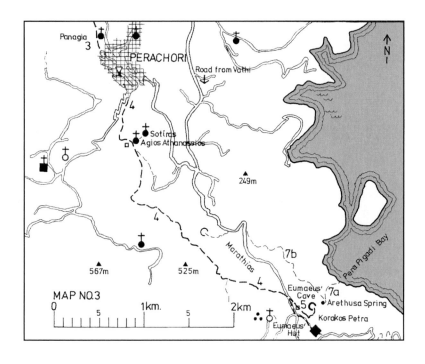

Map no. 3: From Perachori to Eumaeus' Hut and the Korakos Petra

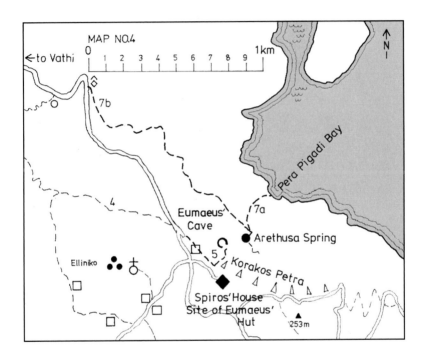

Map no. 4: Walk to Eumaeus' Cave, Arethusa Spring and Pera Pigadi

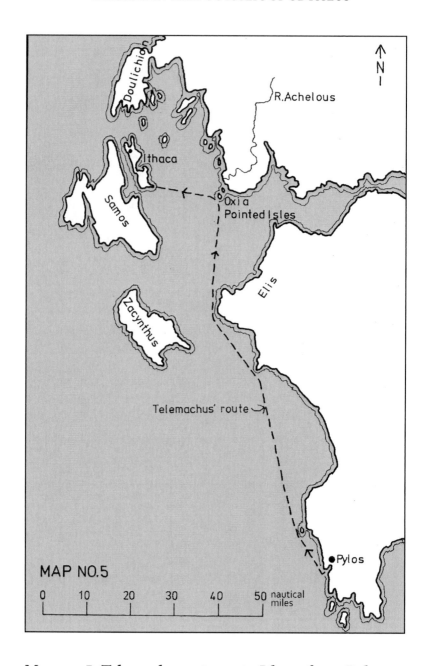

Map no. 5: Telemachus returns to Ithaca from Pylos

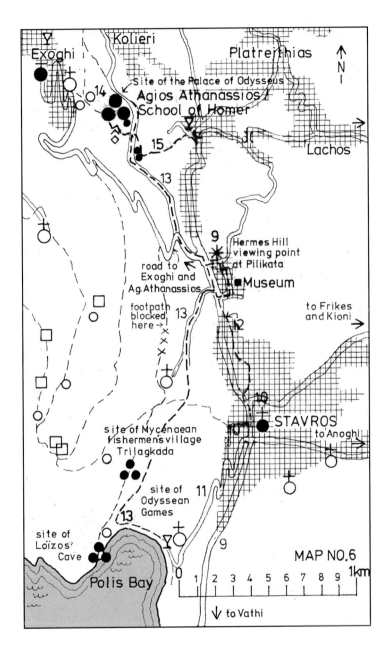

Map no. 6: Polis Bay, Stavros and the Palace of Odysseus

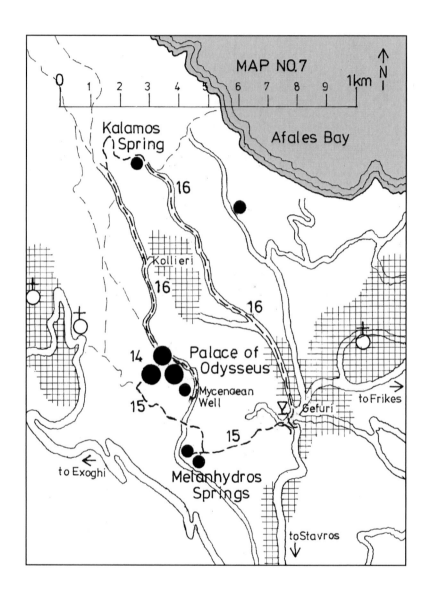

Map no. 7: Approaches to the Palace of Odysseus

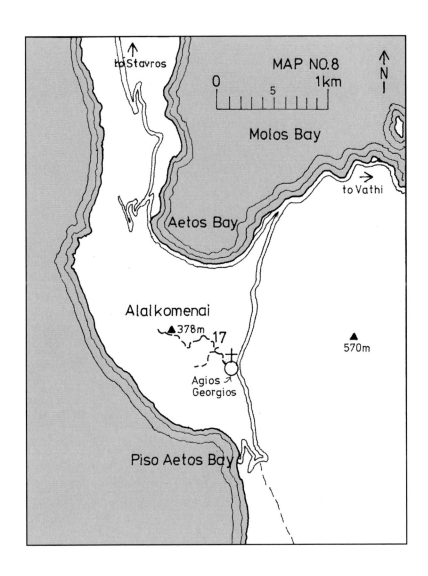

Map no. 8: The Acropolis of Alalkomenai

When the brightest of all stars

came up, the star which often

ushers in the light of early Dawn,

the ship's voyage was done and she

drew near to Ithaca.

The Odyssey, Book 13: 93-95

For the story of Odysseus' arrival back in Ithaca please read
The Odyssey, Book 13: 38–441

1

Odysseus returns home to Ithaca

See map no.2, page 15

Walk from Vathi harbour around to the coastal hamlet of Dexia, or Dexa on the Topo map. This bay is situated immediately to the north-west of Vathi, soon after you pass the petrol station. There you will find a shallow-sloping and surprisingly sandy beach, sheltered by its position at the end of the Gulf of Molos and enclosed by two projecting headlands. You can go there by car or scooter if you wish.

According to Homer Odysseus set off for Troy with 12 ships fully manned by men from his kingdom, which covered the modern islands of Ithaca, Kefalonia and Zakynthos and a small area of the mainland opposite the islands. He lost all his ships and all his men and, 20 years later, he returned alone.

Odysseus was brought back to Ithaca in a ship belonging to King Alcinous of Phaeacia, thought to be modern Corfu. Homer described his arrival:

When the brightest of all stars came up, the star which often ushers in the light of early Dawn, the ship's voyage was done and she drew near to Ithaca.

Now in that island is a cove named Phorcys, the Old Man of the Sea, with two projecting headlands sheer to seaward but sloping down on the side of the harbour. They protect it from the heavy swell raised by rough weather in the open and allow large ships to ride inside without tying up, once they are within mooring distance of the shore.

(13: 93-102)

The cove 'named Phorcys, the Old Man of the Sea' is said to be the harbour of Dexia. Looking out from this harbour you will see 'two projecting headlands sheer to seaward but sloping down on the side of the harbour'. These headlands, and the Gulf of Molos beyond them, protect the harbour from 'the heavy swell raised by rough weather'.

It was here that the Phaeacians put in, knowing the place; and such was the headway of the ship, rowed by those able hands, that a full half of her keel's length mounted the beach.

(13: 113-115)

Most of Ithaca's beaches are steep and pebbly. It is unusual to find a relatively sandy beach with a shallow slope where a full half of a ship's keel could be rowed ashore and mount the beach without damage, but here it is!

The beach at Dexia has remained largely unaltered over the course of time, but these days it has a small wall built along the shoreline to protect it, and several rows of olive trees planted behind it. It is so protected and shallow-sloping that modern houses have been built along the back of it.

The present-day holiday accommodation known as Forkis Apartments sits right behind the beach at Dexia. The proprietors gave it this name because 'Forkis is the old name for this area – this is what people used to call it'.

They say the place was definitely called Forkis before it was called Dexia, and that there is a long tradition for that name.

Dexia beach

In Homer's story Odysseus fell asleep on the journey back from Phaeacia. When their ship arrived at the *'harbour named Phorcys'* the sailors lifted him ashore and left him, still asleep *'with his sheet and glossy rug',* on the shore. Then they unloaded the treasures that the king, queen and nobles of Phaeacia had given him, and piled them under an olive tree away from the path, in case some passer-by stole them. The Phaeacian sailors then left for home.

The generous Phaeacians had given Odysseus *'countless gifts of bronze, gold and woven stuffs'* including (and it is important to remember these) 13 bronze tripod-lebetes. (For more about tripod-lebetes see Chapter 12, pages 91-93.)

It was misty when Odysseus woke up, and the landscape of Ithaca with its *'long hill-paths, welcoming bays, beetling rocks and leafy trees'* seemed unfamiliar to him. As you look around you in Ithaca you will immediately notice that this description precisely fits the landscape. The long hill-paths, the many bays to welcome a small boat, the overhanging (beetling) rocks and leafy trees are all particular features of this island. But Odysseus had no idea where he was.

First he checked his pile of treasure and found that nothing was missing, then the goddess Athena approached him. Throughout *The Odyssey* Odysseus' guardian the goddess Athena disguised herself in different ways, and now she appeared as a handsome young shepherd. When Odysseus failed to recognise the island and asked the name of it, she continued to describe the place in her reply:

> *"Sir... you must be a simpleton or have travelled very far from your home to ask me what this country is. It has a name by no means inglorious. In fact it is known to thousands, to all the peoples who live in the direction of dawn and sunrise and all who live in the other direction, towards the twilight West. True, it is rugged and unfit for driving horses and though not extensive it is very far from poor. Corn grows well and there is wine too. Rain and fresh dew are never lacking; and it has excellent pasture for goats and cattle, timber of all kinds, and watering places that never fail. And so, my friend, the name of Ithaca has travelled even as far as Troy."*
> (13: 235-249)

Ithaca is, indeed, a rugged and rocky little island, quite unfit for a horse-drawn carriage. Yet there is enough rain and dew for its people to grow corn and tend their vineyards, and to keep goats and cattle. Its hills are still thick with trees and it has freshwater springs that never fail.

So can we be sure that Homer envisaged Odysseus' arrival at Dexia Bay? Some scholars have suggested that the harbour where Odysseus arrived might have been at neighbouring Vathi, or at Polis Bay in the north of the island. Polis Bay, as its name (City Bay) suggests, was the harbour associated with the main town of Ithaca at that time. If their king had arrived at this harbour one of his people would have immediately spotted him. I believe that Homer's narrative required Odysseus to arrive discreetly at a port where his boat could sneak in unseen. This would have been possible either at Dexia or at Vathi way back around 1200BC, when there was no town in either place. Although Vathi means 'deep', old engravings, made before the modern harbour was built up, show the beach there with a shallow slope similar to that of Dexia. Also, as Vathi has a quite exceptional natural harbour, the Phaeacian sailors would have known it, just as Homer describes. Until we have more evidence I think we have to leave this question open. In Homer's story Odysseus could have arrived either at Dexia or at Vathi harbour. Dexia still fits his description well and back in Homer's day (around the 8th century BC) Vathi probably fitted his words equally.

"This is the broad vaulted cavern

where you made many potent

sacrifices to the Nymphs.

The forest-clad slopes behind are

those of Mount Neriton."

The Odyssey, Book 13: 349-351

The goddess Athena brings Odysseus to the Cave of the Nymphs.

2

To the Cave of the Nymphs

See map no.2, page 15

On the road northwards out of Vathi, just after the petrol station and before you reach Dexia, there is a winding road running up to the Cave of the Nymphs, which is also called Marmarospilio (Marble Cave in Greek). At the beginning of this road there is a large and discouraging sign saying ΣΠΗΛΑΙΟ ΝΥΜΦΩΝ ΚΛΕΙΣΤΟ ΝΥΜΡΗ CAVE CLOSED. Unfortunately it isn't possible to enter the cave at present but, even so, it is well worth a visit. If you are starting in Dexia, or if you have a car or scooter, press on about 3.6km uphill up this modern winding road until you reach the cave. If you would like to go up to the Cave of the Nymphs on foot it is best to take route 2a (below) from Vathi.

The goddess Athena then suggested to Odysseus that they hide his treasure in a *'pleasant hazy cavern sacred to the nymphs'*, and he agreed. Odysseus and the goddess then walked from *'the cove named Phorcys, the Old Man of the Sea'* to the Cave of the Nymphs.

I hate to say this but it is also difficult to be sure, when you arrive, that you have reached the right spot. The sign, placed to the right-hand side of the road, is damaged and illegible. It almost feels as if there is a conspiracy to prevent you looking at this important ancient site.

Damaged sign at the Cave of the Nymphs

To reach the Cave of the Nymphs from the small parking area adjacent to the road head up a short steep path next to this sign to the cave. First you pass a footpath to the left signed to Perachori and marked by the Avenza Trails of Ithaca team with a post and their particular blue and white markings. Continue on past this footpath to a small terrace of flat ground in front of the main entrance to the cave.

But is this truly the Cave of the Nymphs that Homer describes? According to the Homeric specialist Professor John V Luce, sherds picked up in the cave mouth showed that dedications were made here to the nymphs in Hellenistic times, between 323 and 31BC. Inside the cave a squared block of stone that was described as an altar by Lord Rennell of Rodd, who personally funded the British archaeological team in the 1930s and wrote a book about it, can still be seen. When the floor of the cave was excavated in the 1980s by the American archaeologist Sarantis Symeonoglou, he also found votive offerings from the time of Odysseus that related it directly to the worship of nymphs, and the bones of many deer given in sacrifice. Unfortunately his team, by digging down deeply below the floor of the cave, damaged some stalagmite columns from inside the cave. They set the pieces into cement above and to the left of the main entrance door to the cave, where they can still be seen today.

When Odysseus and the goddess arrived at the entrance to the cave she lifted the mist and showed Odysseus his country saying:

And now, to convince you, let me show you the Ithacan scene, Here is the harbour of Phorcys, the Old Man of the Sea; and there at the head of the harbour is the long-leaved olive tree, and near by the pleasant hazy cave that is sacred to the Nymphs whom men call Naiads. This is the broad vaulted cavern where you made many potent sacrifices to the Nymphs. The forest-clad slopes behind are those of Mount Neriton.

(13: 344-351)

View of Mount Neriton from the Cave of the Nymphs

You can stand in front of the Cave of the Nymphs and look out over the bays of Dexia at the slopes of Mount Neriton (or Νήριτο) opposite.

At 809m Neriton is the highest mountain in Ithaca. Its lower slopes are still densely covered in bushes although they may not be quite as '*forest-clad*' as they were in the days of Homer.

Odysseus was overjoyed to find that he had reached his homeland at last. He kissed the soil, lifted his hands in greeting and prayed to the nymphs. Meanwhile, the goddess Athena plunged down into the gloom of the cavern to find a suitable corner to hide the treasure.

At present there is a padlocked metal gate across this entrance.

> *The cave has two mouths. The one that looks north is the way down for men.*
>
> (13: 109-110)

When the cave was open you could enter through the narrow north-facing entrance 'for men' onto a platform in the rock about 2m wide and 6m long. From here a set of narrow and slippery steps, cut into the rock, descend about 3m into the main 'vaulted' part of the cave. Its base is roughly circular and about 6m high and 6m in diameter. The light here is indeed 'hazy' as it is lit only by a hole in the 'broad-vaulted' roof high above, as described in the extract from Book 13: 344-351 quoted on page 31 above. At the base of the cave there are also some adjoining smaller chambers where treasure could be hidden. When Odysseus and the goddess had hidden the gold and bronze objects and the fine fabrics, she closed the entrance with a stone. You can imagine how the narrow north-facing entrance 'for men' could (if you were strong enough to move it) be closed with a single stone.

The north facing entrance, for men, to the Cave of the Nymphs

Homer goes on to describe the second entrance:

The other, facing south, is for the gods; and as immortals come in by this way men do not trespass there.

(13: 110-112)

At the Cave of the Nymphs there is a second '*entrance*' in the roof for the '*immortals to come in by this way*'.

To look down into the cave through the 'south-facing entrance for immortals' descend the path outside the cave a few yards and you will find a small steep track up to the right. This will bring you to the top of

the hole in the roof that lights the cave.

Odysseus and the goddess Athena then sat outside the cave by the trunk of a sacred olive tree. Together they discussed the downfall of the presumptuous suitors who were courting Odysseus' wife, Penelope. The suitors wanted to take over Odysseus' kingdom and, to ensure success, they were also plotting to murder his only son, Telemachus.

The goddess advised Odysseus to go first to visit his loyal swineherd:

> 'You must first of all go to the swineherd in charge of your pigs...you will find him watching over his swine out at the pastures by the Raven's Crag and at the Spring of Arethousa.'
>
> (13: 403-4 and 406-7)

She said that the swineherd Eumaeus lived 'at the extreme limit of his land' and 'a long way from the city'. (17: 25)

At this time, according to Homer, Odysseus' son, Telemachus, was on the mainland Peloponnese trying to find out what had happened to his father. Before the goddess Athena left to fetch Telemachus, she disguised Odysseus as an elderly beggar:

> She withered the smooth skin on his supple limbs, robbed his head of its dark locks, covered his whole body with an old man's wrinkles, and dimmed the brightness of his fine eyes. And she changed his clothing into a shabby cloak and tunic, filthy rags grimy with smoke. Over his back she threw a large and well-worn hide of a nimble stag; and finally she gave him a staff and a poor, shabby knapsack with a shoulder strap.
>
> (13: 429-438)

She did this, she said, to make him both unrecognisable and *'repulsive to the whole gang of Suitors and even to your wife and the son you left at home'.*

And how did she do this? Well, Homer was a wonderful storyteller and Athena was a goddess!

2a

If you prefer to walk up from Vathi to the Cave of the Nymphs this walk, which is just over 2km, is marked '3' on the Topo map. It takes about an hour walking uphill at moderate speed. The path is clear and well marked.

This is the way to go: On entering Vathi from the north you will find, at the junction with the road around the harbour of Vathi, the Odyssey Diving-Sea Kayak Club. You will see the club opposite you, with pale blue walls and bright yellow doors, next to the turn-off to Perachori. Head along the road running inland towards Perachori, which is also marked ΟΔΟΣ ΠΗΝΕΛΟΠΗΣ PINELOPIS. Take a right-hand turn from this road where it is signed Matrata. Follow the winding road towards Matrata until you reach a church with a graveyard on the outer side of a hairpin bend. On the inner side of the bend, opposite the church, you will find a Trails of Ithaca sign on a post with blue and white markings. This path, which is marked as the beginning of walk no.3 on the Topo map, is where you should begin your walk.

Follow the blue and white signs on foot and you will finally arrive at a narrow tarmac road, and directly opposite you will see the damaged sign and the path up to Marmarospilio/ Cave of the Nymphs.

2b

To descend from Marmarospilio/Cave of the Nymphs to Vathi you can, of course, return on the same path. This alternative route is slightly rougher and narrower in places. This path is about 1.6km downhill until you reach a large locked church above the main square in Vathi. This downhill walk takes about an hour walking at a moderate speed.

From the path directly up to the Cave of the Nymphs, above the tarmac road, start off on the footpath towards Perachori going uphill, sometimes on steps, until you reach a little white-painted church. At the church take the lower path (not the upper path to Perachori) and then descend 0.3km. The path eventually turns down to your left – where it was recently widened by building work taking place, and meets a tarmac road. Go left along the tarmac road for a short distance. On your right, behind a large carob tree, there is a path leading immediately, and straight in front of you, to a locked gate. Ignore this gate, but turn to the right in front of it and you will see the path to follow running along by the fence. Eventually you arrive at a large threshing floor. Tracks are visible going to left and right from the threshing floor. Take the path to the right and continue down along this unmarked track until you reached a paved and stepped footpath into the centre of Vathi. There is quite a maze of paths in this area, but you should not get lost now as the harbour of Vathi can be clearly seen.

After hiding his treasure in the Cave of the Nymphs Odysseus set out for Eumaeus' Hut. If you follow these walks in sequence, in the footsteps of Odysseus, it will be your next destination as well.

"You must first of all go to the swineherd in charge of your pigs… you will find him watching over his swine out at the pastures by the Raven's Crag and at the Spring of Arethousa."

The Odyssey, Book 13: 403-4 and 406-7

The goddess Athena directs Odysseus to visit the swineherd Eumaeus.

3

From the Cave of the Nymphs to Perachori

See map no.2, page 15

This walk follows the first part of Odysseus' walk towards the Marathias Plain, Eumaeus' Hut and the Korakos Petra. The walk is quite easy with magnificent views. It is clear and well-marked, both on the Topo and the Avenza maps, but it is uphill nearly all the way from Marmarospilio to Perachori. On the Topo map it is part of walk no.3. The distance each way is 1.95km. The walk takes about an hour uphill to Perachori walking at a moderate speed. The downhill return journey is quicker.

To set out on foot for the place where Eumaeus' Hut once stood, leave the Cave of the Nymphs and take the footpath signed to Perachori. Continue uphill, sometimes on steps, until you reach a small white church then take the upper path towards Perachori. Walk uphill past old water sternas and threshing floors until finally you descend into Perachori.

View to the north over Vathi

Scholars believe that Homer envisaged Odysseus taking this path when he left the Cave of the Nymphs on his way to visit Eumaeus. He describes how Odysseus:

> ...*followed a rough track leading through the woods and up to the hills towards the place where Athene had told him he would meet the worthy swineherd, who of all the servants Odysseus had acquired had shown himself to be the most faithful steward of his property.*
>
> (14: 1 - 5)

In Ithaca the old towns were built on the high ground to escape the pirates who infested the seas until the 18th century AD when the Venetians managed to clear them. Perachori is the old town on the high ground above Vathi. Your track will bring you into Perachori by the old church of Panagia, at a hairpin bend on a tarmac road with a blue and white sign. On this road turn downhill and then directly onwards you will discover, on the right-hand side, a café Βεράντα στο Ιόνιο (Veranda onto the Ionian). This is a good resting place with wonderful views. To continue onwards towards Eumaeus' little home continue on the same road past the café.

Homer envisaged Odysseus walking along this path to the house where his loyal swineherd lived and where, after 20 years, he would finally meet up with the son he last saw as a baby. Later he would walk this path in the opposite direction with Eumaeus in order to reach the palace at Agios Athanasios / School of Homer in the north of the island.

Eumaeus lived

'at the extreme limit of his land'

and

'a long way from the city.'

The Odyssey, Book 17: 25

4

From Perachori to Eumaeus' Hut
by the Korakos Petra

See map no.3, page 16

The distance of this walk is just over 4km each way, and the path is not always easy. It will take about 2 hours each way. There is no sustenance at the far end so, unless you have arranged for a pick-up there, you will need to walk back along the same route. It is a good idea to take the Topo map, the Avenza map on a fully charged smartphone, a bottle of water and a stick. You may need all of these.

You can pick up this path at the café Βεράντα στο Ιόνιο (Veranda onto the Ionian) in Perachori. To make your way onwards towards the site of Eumaeus' Hut continue southwards along this road. Where the road is marked Monasteri Taxiarchon carry straight on until, at the far side of a hairpin bend, you will see an Avenza Trails of Ithaca post marking the second part of the path from Perachori to the Marathias Plain, Eumaeus' Hut and the Korakos Petra. Take this path, which is marked Marathias 3.6km. Follow the blue and white markings made by the Avenza mapping team.

For the first part of this walk the path leads through the woods. Just as

Homer describes, it is '*a rough track leading through the woods and up to the hills*'. 700m after the path begins take the right-hand upper fork marked Marathias by Avenza. You will pass a water sterna and a small church on your left-hand side. The path here is clear, but rocky. It has deteriorated in places, so a stick is useful. After about 2.5km the woods begin to clear and you find yourself on stony open ground with bushes. The second part of this path takes you about 1.8km down onto the Marathias Plain. The views here are beautiful, but keep a sharp eye out for the blue and white Avenza markings as, at times, the path can look very similar to a goat track. If you haven't seen the markings for a while, and the track is still unclear, it could be that you've gone off-piste. Check your position with the Avenza map and, if this is the case, retrace your steps until you are on track again. As you reach the Marathias Plain you will pass some dumped cars and finally you will find a parking place next to a large black water tank. Here you will meet the road from Vathi, which is by now a dirt track.

If you have not arranged a pick-up here you will need to follow this route in reverse. Watch carefully for the blue and white markings in the first part of this track. Finally, when you reach the rather poor tarmac road down into Perachori take the right-hand downward fork into the town. After 540m you will be happy to find the café Βεράντα στο Ιόνιο (Veranda onto the Ionian) and its proprietor Spiridoula there to serve you.

After reaching the Marathias Plain, Odysseus (who was a great deal tougher than most of us) went on to see the swineherd Eumaeus. I suggest that we lesser mortals drive down to this place by car or scooter before making the other walks I describe here.

If you have a car or scooter, drive down to the Marathias Plain to look at Eumaeus' Hut and the Raven's Crag (or Korakos Petra as it is known in Greek). Homer envisaged this place, about 5km to the south of Vathi, as the home of Odysseus' loyal swineherd Eumaeus.

From the sea-front at Vathi, turn up the street marked ΟΔΟΣ ΕΥΜΑΙΟΥ (Eumaeus' Street) in Greek and EYMAIOU in English lettering, which is also signed 'Νοσοκομείο Hospital Αστυνομία Police'. Follow this road onwards, turning neither to right nor left, until you reach your destination. The final stretch of the road is a dirt track, but it is drivable. When you come to a fork in the track (the left fork goes in the direction of Eumaeus' Cave, and the right fork to Agios Ioannis) there is a small parking place to the right-hand side next to a large black water tank. Leave your vehicle here and continue on foot.

You will remember that the goddess advised Odysseus to go first to visit Eumaeus, who lived 'at the extreme limit of his land' and 'a long way from the city' (17: 25) The city, in Odysseus' time, was on the western slopes of Stavros, in the north of Ithaca.

Continue southwards along the dirt road to the place where the present-day 'Eumaeus' still lives.

Spiros is a traditional Ithacan shepherd who lives at the top of the Korakos Petra. His family have owned this land for generations. He lives in the old style with his 40 long-tailed Ithacan sheep, his two dogs, his many cats and chickens, and his flock of geese. The land around his house is not fenced but it is private property, so please proceed with caution and respect. Ideally you should go with someone who speaks reasonable Greek.

In *The Odyssey Book 14* Homer describes how Odysseus arrived at the house of Eumaeus who was '*watching over his swine out at their pastures by the Raven's Crag and at the Spring of Arethousa*' (13: 407-408)

As you walk towards Spiros' house the land becomes more agricultural and scattered with strange rounded rocks.

Odysseus found Eumaeus '*sitting in the porch of his hut in the farmyard, whose high walls, perched on an eminence and protected by a clearing, enclosed a fine and spacious courtyard*'. (14: 7-9)

Spiros' small house is set next to a large courtyard surrounded by trees. Homer described how Eumaeus lived right next to the high precipice of the Korakos Petra and Spiros' house is built in much the same spot.

In Homer's story, as Odysseus arrived at Eumaeus' Hut, four savage dogs leaped out and flew at him. He sat down and dropped his staff so as not to enrage them further. Their barking raised Eumaeus, who threw a shower of stones to disperse them.

Luckily, although Spiros' two dogs are a bit ragged, they are quiet and very friendly. They are called by Ottoman names – Sultana and Bey. However around the back of the house he also (like Penelope at the Palace of Odysseus) keeps a flock of geese, and these may be fiercer.

Spiros' house stands right next to, and above, the massive crag of the Korakos Petra.

Spiros' geese

The English Raven's Crag is Κόρακος Πέτρα (Korakos Petra) in Greek, but this is an understatement. When you arrive you will find it is not a 'crag' or a 'rock' but a massive 200ft-high cliff spanning right across the top of a wide and steep-sided ravine that runs down to the sea at Pera Pigadi Bay. Halfway down is an ancient spring of sweet water that never dries called Arethusa Spring. The name Pera Pigadi means 'Far Away Well'.

In *The Odyssey* the swineherd Eumaeus welcomed the stranger into his hut. Although he did not see through Odysseus' disguise he shared fresh pork and wine with him and they sat down to swap stories of their lives. Odysseus was known to be clever, crafty and somewhat duplicitous and, as he didn't want Eumaeus to recognise him, he made up a yarn, pretending that he came from Crete. He told Eumaeus that he had met Odysseus, that he knew that he was still alive, and that he would soon return home to reclaim his kingdom. The stories that Eumaeus told in return were true, unlike those of Odysseus. However while Eumaeus believed all the lies that

47

Odysseus told he did not believe the one true thing he said:

> *'I will not merely state that Odysseus is coming back, I will swear to it...*
> *This very month Odysseus will be here. Between the waning of the old*
> *moon and the waxing of the new, he will come back to his home and will*
> *punish all who dishonour his wife and his noble son.'*

(14: 150-151 and 161-164)

Eumaeus replied that this would never happen, but Odysseus in disguise insisted saying:

> *If... your master does not return as I say he will, you shall tell your men to*
> *throw me over a precipice.*

(14: 399-400)

The cliff of the Korakos Petra or Raven's Crag

As you stand in front of Spiros' house, just above the cliff of the Korakos Petra, you can imagine Odysseus there and you can easily understand how real this threat would feel.

Between the cliff and the house stands an ancient circular enclosure built in rough fieldstones. Spiros doesn't use it, but his father used to pen his goats in there. When Professor John V Luce came here in 1975 this animal pen was topped with spiny brushwood. In *The Odyssey*, Homer describes how Eumaeus built enclosures for his sows and piglets with rough fieldstones topped with hedges of wild pear:

> *The herdsman had made it himself for his absent master's swine...building a wall of the quarried stone with a hedge of wild pear on top.*
>
> (14: 8-11)

But the swineherd was unwilling

to sleep there away from his boars.

He got himself ready for a night

outside… and so he went off to pass

the night where the white-tusked

boars slept, under an overhanging

rock sheltered from the

northerly winds.

The Odyssey, Book 14: 522-523 and 531-532

5

Down beside the Korakos Petra to Eumaeus' Cave

See map no.4, page 17

This is a walk down beside the northern end of the Korakos Petra to Eumaeus' Cave. From Spiros' home you can now return to the point where the track divides at a Y-junction. Alternatively, if you parked in the small parking space by the big black water tank, you can start your walk from here. Take the track signed to Eumaeus' Cave. The track down to the cave is steep, slippery and not simple to find. Wear appropriate shoes or boots and consider taking a stick. Distance: 500m each way. Time: allow 25 minutes down to the caves and 15 minutes to return.

Following the signs towards Eumaeus' Cave you will come first to a concrete bunker, probably left from the Second World War, covered in graffiti. Much of the graffiti is rude but the bunker is a very good landmark. From here walk southwards past a concrete water catchment tank along an unclear path until, going down the side of the Korakos Petra, you find a small gate. From here onwards the path is clearly marked with blue and white signs put in place by the Avenza mapping team, but you still need to take care and stay alert.

Homer describes how Odysseus (who was still in disguise) and Eumaeus swapped tales until, as evening fell, Eumaeus prepared a bed by the fire for his guest. He spread it with the skins of sheep and goats and covered Odysseus with a thick cloak. Then, taking a sharp javelin to ward off attack, Eumaeus went off to spend the night outside:

And so he went off to pass the night where the white-tusked boars slept, under an overhanging rock sheltered from the northerly winds.

(14: 531-532.)

View of the Korakos Petra from the inside of Eumaeus' Cave

After a bit you will find plenty of overhanging rocks on a south-facing rock face giving shelter from the northerly winds, and not one but three caves where Eumaeus might have slept. The first cave, at the level of the path, is large and feels damp but one can imagine a swineherd spending the night there. Farther on there is another cave, equally spacious and completely dry, where there would be room for a swineherd along with quite a few white-tusked boars.

High up in between the two large caves is a third and much smaller cave; the climb up to it is tricky but doable. This cave could serve as a lookout post as there is a good view across to the Korakos Petra and down to the small bay of Pera Pigadi.

The bright-eyed goddess stood near him and said: "Telemachus, it is wrong of you to linger abroad and leave your property unguarded with such a rabble in your house... urge your host, Menelaus of the loud war-cry, to let you go at once."

The Odyssey, Book 15: 9-11 and 13-14

6

Telemachus returns from Pylos to Ithaca

See map no.5, page 18

From the top of the Korakos Petra you will have looked down the ravine to Pera Pigadi Bay and, in seeking out Eumaeus' Cave, you will have made your way down the steep slope to the north side of the cliff. But to reach Pera Pigadi Bay, in the footsteps of Telemachus, you will need to go by boat.

For Homer's story to work well he needed Odysseus to meet his son,

Telemachus, somewhere far from his palace, in a place where they would not be spotted by anyone who might spread the word back to the suitors. He arranged that they should meet at Eumaeus' Hut. However, at the time of Odysseus' return to Ithaca Telemachus had gone to visit his father's colleagues in the Trojan War, to try to get news of him.

After she left Odysseus at the Cave of the Nymphs, the goddess Athena went off on her own to fetch Telemachus. She found him in Sparta at the house of King Menelaus and the beautiful Queen Helen who, according to Homer, was the cause of the Trojan War. The goddess then told Telemachus to set out immediately to return to Ithaca and, after an extended farewell and the offering of many gifts, Telemachus returned to Pylos. There he had left his ship in the beautiful Bay of Navarino near the palace of the great King Nestor. Homer described Telemachus' journey home carefully.

It was late afternoon when Telemachus and his crew set sail. The goddess had warned him of the suitors' plan to murder him on his return saying:

> 'And here's another matter for you to bear in mind. The ringleaders among the suitors are lying in ambush in the straits between Ithaca and the rugged coast of Samos, intent on murdering you before you can reach home.'
> (15: 26-30)

Samos, or Same, is the ancient name of the modern island of Kefalonia. Thus the 'straits between Ithaca and the rugged coast of Samos' can be identified as the Ithaca Channel. The suitors lay in wait near the small island of Asteris, or Dascalio, that lies off Polis Bay in this strait.

In order to avoid this ambush the goddess Athena instructed the young man to sail under cover of darkness, to keep close to the mainland shore avoiding his father's islands, and to disembark at the first point of Ithaca that he reached:

> 'Steer your ship well clear of the islands, and sail on through the night: your guardian god will send you a following breeze. Land in Ithaca at the first point you reach and send the ship and the whole ship's company round to the harbour, but before you yourself do anything else, visit the swineherd in charge of your pigs, who is loyal to you in spite of everything. Stay there for the night and send him to the city to give your wise mother, Penelope, the news that you are back from Pylos and safe.'
>
> (15: 33-41)

Telemachus and his crew left the harbour and, hugging the shore, sailed past the fertile landscape of Crouni and Chalcis. The sun set and darkness fell. The night was clear but moonless. Then Telemachus sailed past Elis and set his course for the Pointed Isles:

> Telemachus set a course for the Pointed Isles, wondering whether he would get through alive or be caught.
>
> (15: 299-300)

The 'pointed' or 'sharp' isles are also known as the Oxeiai or Thoai islands. In this time before maps they made a good landmark for the sailor as they are, in fact, conical in shape with rather pointed summits. They stand at the southern end of the Echinades by the delta of the River Achelous, and can easily be seen from Ithaca. The outer island is now called Oxia.

From here Telemachus and his crew, following the instructions of the goddess, headed for the 'first point you reach' or the 'first foreland of Ithaca'. This is the rocky headland in the south of Ithaca now known as

Cape Mounta. There is no landing place on the cape, but immediately to the north is Pera Pigadi Bay (see detailed Map No.4, p.16). On arrival Telemachus and his men anchored their boat, jumped out onto the beach, and prepared a meal, which they drank with sparkling wine. Then Athena's instructions were to:

> 'send the ship and the whole ship's company round to the harbour'
>
> (15: 35-36)

Telemachus obeyed the goddess precisely. After their meal on the beach he gave his ship's crew the following instructions:

> 'Take the ship round to the city,' he said, 'while I pay a visit to the farms and herdsmen.'
>
> (15: 501-502)

The Homeric scholar John V Luce, who carefully followed the sea route made by Telemachus, believed that the route then taken by his crew was up the east coast of Ithaca, around the north of the island, then southwards 'round to the city', which was situated inland from Polis Bay. Meanwhile Telemachus set out to walk up to the little house of Eumaeus the swineherd at the top of the Korakos Petra.

As the upper part of the path from Pera Pigadi Bay to the top of the Korakos Petra is now broken it has been suggested that Telemachus might have landed at Antri Bay which is quite a bit farther around the south of Ithaca. In the 19th century AD this bay was used for loading and unloading of the currants that were grown on the Marathias Plain. A few ruined buildings can still be seen there. The actual bay where Telemachus landed is not described by Homer, so Antri Bay is a possible alternative to Pera Pigadi;

however it is much farther away from the Korakos Petra so I feel that Pera Pigadi is a more likely candidate. As you will see from our description of the walk up from Pera Pigadi (Walk No.7b, Chapter 7, page 66) there are signs of several ancient paths right up to the top of the cliff. I believe that, back in the days of Odysseus, a fit young man like Telemachus could have made light work of the path from Pera Pigadi up to the top of the Korakos Petra.

Telemachus set off on foot and walked at a good pace till he reached the yard where his large droves of pigs were kept and where his swineherd slept among them.

The Odyssey, Book 15: 551-557

7

Pera Pigadi Bay, Arethusa Spring and the Korakos Petra

See map no.4, page 17

To reach Pera Pigadi Bay, in the footsteps of Telemachus, you will need to go by boat. From there we believe Telemachus made his way up to Eumaeus' Hut by taking a route around the southern end of the Korakos Petra.

We hired a boat with a skipper from Vathi and the cost for the round trip was €100 including petrol. There are websites for two boat hire companies in Vathi. They have several names, but my impression is that they cooperate together. The names are Odyssey Outdoor Activities (tel: 00 30 69481 82655) Odyssey Sea Kayaking, Odyssey Boats, Ithaca Boats or Rent-a-Boat Ithaca (tel: 00 30 69490 35670 or info@rentaboatithaca.com). You will find contact forms on their websites.

Our skipper was extremely helpful with the landing. He jumped overboard and pulled the boat as near the shore as he safely could. However it was still necessary to wade ashore in a swimsuit holding any other kit above the water.

As I explained in my description of Telemachus' journey back from Pylos I believe that Homer envisaged Telemachus landing at the beach at Pera Pigadi Bay. From there he would have walked up the steep ravine to Eumaeus' Hut at the top of the Korakos Petra where he would meet his father for the first time in 20 years.

'Telemachus set off on foot and walked at a good pace till he reached the yard where his large droves of pigs were kept and where his swineherd slept among them.'

(15: 554-557)

Dawn was breaking as he reached Eumaeus' Hut. Eumaeus' dogs rushed up to him wagging their tails as they knew Telemachus well. The swineherd was overjoyed to see the young man safely home and introduced him to the stranger, who was in fact his father, Odysseus, in disguise.

'In the hut Odysseus and the worthy swineherd were now preparing their breakfast in the dawn light, after stirring up the fire, and sending the herdsmen off with the pigs to the pastures. As Telemachus approached the hut the baying dogs began wagging their tails, but they did not bark.'

(16: 1-5)

7a

To walk from Pera Pigadi Bay up as far as the Arethusa Spring there is currently a good clear path marked with blue and white signs. It is

a fairly steep uphill walk of about 350m that takes about 15 minutes. From Arethusa Spring up to the top of the cliff there is no current footpath. You will need to take the walk that I describe in 7b below, back to the rest stop or picnic shelter on the Vathi road.

My walk-checker setting off from Pera Pigadi towards the top of the Korakos Petra

I do believe, however, that the route directly up this gulley was the one that Homer envisaged Telemachus walking. In years gone by, before they were destroyed by earthquakes, I believe that there were several footpaths leading up to, and around, the southern end of the Korakos Petra. To prove that it would have been possible back in the days of Odysseus, my walk-checker decided to carry on up to the top around the southern side of the cliff. I didn't go with him and I advise against it. If anyone else does this I take absolutely no responsibility for their safety.

But to prove it is possible I include his report here:

> *"Arethusa Spring itself is a shady and lovely spot, with plentiful clear and clean water in a natural well, down in the right-hand corner of the place as you approach from below. There were two old buckets – one on a piece of slender rope – by the side of it. But both were damaged. The one without the rope was completely rusted and you would have to be very thirsty to want to drink water that had been in it. The other was in better condition, but a section of its bottom was rusted through. You could drop it into the well and haul out water, but you had to be quick to get a few mouthfuls because it was leaking on its way back to ground level.*

Arethusa Spring

"I managed after half a dozen lowerings to get enough water into a plastic bottle to take with me for a drink or possibly two. But the bottle and I were soon to part company.

"Behind the area of the spring, the rock wall becomes almost perpendicular. There is no path of any sort and there are barely any footholds or handholds. One also needs to get over to the left of the spring area to make the ascent, which means you get closer to being over a sheer drop down to the bottom of the ravine – at a distance downward which is difficult to calculate, since it's not possible to see through the tops of the trees below. It was while going up a series of rock faces, heading upwards, southwards and eastwards, that the bottle rolled off a ledge where I had tossed it in order to leave both hands free. It bounced down into the ravine like a scene from a mountaineering disaster movie, and disappeared completely from sight.

"These rock faces were probably the toughest bit of the ascent. They took me over to the east side of the ravine to a point where it was possible to step across from west to east – something that it would be impossible to do lower down. After that it was walking, stooping and crawling through the undergrowth and trees, always heading to a point due south of Pera Pigadi island – that was where the mountainside sloped up to meet the southern end of the Korakos Petra. It was nevertheless impossible to see the summit until I was almost on it because of the trees growing almost all the way to the top.

"The surprising thing was that every so often I would move from crawling to stumbling on what looked very much like a path – not just a goat track but a definite path. These path sections would always lead up and round in the direction that I needed to go – but sadly they often didn't last for long.

One of the longest and clearest started near the top of the climb and took me all the way up onto the Marathias Plain and to the track that goes west back towards the road to Vathi.

"The landscape of the ravine has changed over the years as a result of earthquakes but I am convinced that there was once a network of paths used by shepherds that would have given relatively quick and easy access from Marathias to the spring... It would also have been easy to put up wooden ladders or steps to deal with the tricky rock faces just above the spring.

"A fit young man could probably have bounded up in much less than the two hours and 25 minutes it took me to go from the water's edge at Pera Pigadi to the top of Korakos Petra."

My walk-checker was trying to prove a point, but mercifully there is no need for anyone else to make this perilous journey. From the Arethusa Spring there is a clear and well-marked path of some 1.5km back to the Vathi road. The path is not always easy to walk as the surface can be rocky and slippery. It is worth taking a stick and, of course, water and a fully charged mobile phone. As you reach the end it is paved and by the road you will find a roofed picnic shelter.

7b

It is cheaper and easier for landlubbers to approach the Arethusa Spring and Pera Pigadi Bay on foot. This walk begins at the neat

little picnic shelter put up by the EU on the road from Vathi where the sign says 'Arethusa Spring/Korakos Petra'. The path runs along an east-facing hillside, so it can get very hot in the morning. If you wish you can carry on down to Pera Pigadi Bay and cool off with a swim, but unless you have arranged for a pick-up by boat you will have to return along the same route. To reach the beginning of this walk from Vathi harbour you should drive out along Eumaeus' Street (ΟΔΟΣ ΕΥΜΑΙΟΥ in Greek and EYMAIOU in English lettering) which is also signed 'Νοσοκομείο Hospital Αστυνομία Police'. After some 4.5km you will reach, on your left, the picnic shelter and sign at the top of the path. On the Topo map this path is named 1B. The distance as far as the Arethusa Spring is 1.5km (half an hour on foot) with a further 350m (10-minute) steep walk down to Pera Pigadi Bay. The return uphill walk from the beach to the picnic shelter will take longer, allow an hour and a half.

At first this path is paved but it soon deteriorates into a dirt footpath. The path can be clearly seen but the surface is somewhat treacherous in places, and the area is remote. It is advisable to take water, a stick and a fully charged mobile phone.

Coins from the 4th and 3rd centuries BC found in Ithaca and now
in the Archaeological Museum in Vathi

8

Coins at the Archaeological Museum in Vathi

See map no.2, page 15

Unfortunately, as I write in summer 2021, the Archaeological Museum of Vathi is temporarily closed for repairs. I hope it will reopen early in 2022.

While you are in Vathi make sure to visit its Archaeological Museum whose approximate position is marked with an 'M' on Map 2. This museum has a sign outside: 'Ministry of Culture and Sports, Ephorate of Antiquities of Cephalonia, Archaeological Museum'. It contains finds from the southern half of the island while the Archaeological Collection of Stavros contains finds from the north.

In the far room of this museum you will find a glass-topped showcase containing a selection of silver and bronze coins dating from the 4th and 3rd centuries BC. They were mostly found at the City of Aetos, or Alalkomenai, on the isthmus between the north and south parts of the island. They were discovered there during excavation between 1984 and 1999, by an archaeological team under Professor Sarantis Symeonoglou from the Washington University in St Louis.

Some coins show the head of Odysseus, often wearing a pointed traveller's cap (a pilos) on one side of the coin. On the other side is a rooster (the symbol of Ithaca) or the head of the goddess Athena, or a standing male figure. Some had the head of Odysseus and the word IΘA (short for Ithaca) or IΘAKΩN (of the Ithacans) on the same side.

Written records exist of many collections of similar coins made in the 19th century. Several that are held in the Numismatics Department at the British Museum can now be seen online.

This early coinage is proof that, in the 4th and 3rd centuries BC, this particular island was called Ithaca. They also show that, back then, this island and no other was known as the home of the Homeric hero Odysseus.

To follow chapters 9 to 14 inclusive it is best to base yourself in north Ithaca in the small town of Stavros or, in any case, to start your walks from there.

Telemachus said to Eumaeus: "And now, old friend, will you go quickly down and tell my wise mother, Penelope, that she has me safely back from Pylos."

The Odyssey, Book 16: 130-131

9

Eumaeus walks to the Palace of Odysseus and returns via the Hill of Hermes

See map no.6, page 19

We can locate the position of the 'Ridge' or 'Hill of Hermes' where Eumaeus walked. Hermes Hill is the spit of land that forms the northern reaches of Mount Neriton (marked Νήριτο on the Topo map). It extends to Pelikata in the northern reaches of Stavros. I have marked a Viewing Point with a star on map no.6. If you go to this place you will find the ruin of a small church, which stands on the site of a more ancient temple.

On the day following Telemachus' arrival at Eumaeus' Hut he asked the swineherd to go to the palace to reassure his mother, Penelope, that he was safe. Eumaeus set off early.

In Eumaeus' absence Odysseus (with the help of the goddess) revealed himself to his son and they had a rapturous reunion. Then, almost immediately, they began to develop their plan to kill Penelope's suitors. The problem was there were a great many of them. According to Homer there were 108. They came from all the islands of Odysseus' kingdom: Ithaca, Samos (modern Kefalonia) and Zakynthos. The largest number, 51, came from the neighbouring island of Doulichion, which is thought to be modern Lefkas, situated to the north of Ithaca but under a different rule.

The story of the meeting between Telemachus and his father is best read in the original (16: 130-321) so I will concentrate on the walk made by Eumaeus from his house by the Korakos Petra to the Palace of Odysseus sited at Agios Athanasios / School of Homer in the north of the island. This is a round trip of some 28 miles. It is a long walk but not impossible for a healthy and energetic Ithacan shepherd.

Eumaeus set out from his house in the far south of the island to walk to the Palace of Odysseus in the north. When he had nearly reached the palace, he was joined by a messenger from Telemachus' crew. Having delivered his message to Penelope that Telemachus was safely home, Eumaeus had a long walk ahead of him and was anxious to get back. To save time he didn't go into the town (which we can locate on the western slopes of the existing small town of Stavros) but climbed up to the Hill of Hermes.

The important place to locate on this route is the 'Hill of Hermes' described by Homer. This is just to the north and on the same road as the Archaeological Collection of Stavros.

From our Viewing Point on the Hill of Hermes the ground falls away to the north, east and west to a fertile plain where wild pear trees flower in the spring. If you look across the valley to the north-west you will see the site of the Palace of Odysseus at Agios Athanasios / School of Homer. A rock face, separating the two main levels of the site, stands out on a wooded hillside. From here you can also, like Eumaeus, look to the south-west towards Polis

Bay.

The Viewing Point on the Hill of Hermes

You will remember that the plan hatched by Antinous, the leader of the suitors, was to murder Telemachus on his return to Ithaca. He said:

'...*give me a fast ship and a crew of twenty and I'll lie up for him in the straits between Ithaca and the bluffs of Samos, and catch him on his way. And a grim ending there'll be to this sea-trip of his in search of his father.*'

(4: 669-672)

Now Homer described how, from the Hill of Hermes, the swineherd Eumaeus looked down towards Polis Bay and spotted the suitors' ship returning from their failed attempt to intercept and murder Telemachus:

'*She had a crowd of men on board and a whole armoury of shields and two-edged spears. I took it to be them but I couldn't say for certain.'*

(16: 472-476)

In the Ithaca Channel beyond Polis is the small island of Asteris. It is sometimes called by the later Venetian name of Dascalio. Asteris is the only island in the Ithaca Channel that separates Ithaca from Kefalonia, thus *in the straits between Ithaca and the bluffs of Samos*. It lies directly opposite Polis Bay, off the shore of Kefalonia, where it can sometimes shine in the sunlight like a small star. Behind Asteris, on Kefalonia, are two small inlets where an ambush boat could hide. In Homer's story the suitors kept watch by day and by night from the cliffs above these harbours. They were hoping to catch Telemachus on his return journey, but he evaded capture by disembarking in a remote and rural place in the south.

Due to the trees that have grown up you will now need to go round to the right-hand side of our viewing point at the ruined church to see Afales Bay to the north and Frikes Bay to the east.

We can now cross-check the position of Hermes' Hill from another reference in *The Odyssey*. From here the goddess Athena pointed to her ship, which was moored in the harbour of Rheithron (modern Frikes). She said:

'My ship is not berthed near the city, but over there by the open country, in Rheithron Cove, under the woods of Neion.'

(1: 185-186)

Rheithron means 'watercourse' or 'torrent gulley' in Greek. If you go to Frikes you can see the gulley, which takes the water overflow from the site of the Palace of Odysseus at Agios Athanasios / School of Homer. In the summer months the gulley is dry, but after heavy winter rains a torrent of water comes down it and disgorges into the sea.

The torrent gulley near the harbour at Frikes

We must now follow the swineherd Eumaeus back to his hut on the Marathias Plain down in the south of the island. Before he returned that evening the goddess Athena helped Odysseus back into his disguise as a beggar. The following day Telemachus left his father, Odysseus, at Eumaeus' house and made this same walk back up to the palace.

Bronze bust of Odysseus in Stavros main square

10

Stavros

See map no.6, page 19

On a site to the south-west of the main square at Stavros limited archaeological excavations were undertaken in 1937, 1944 and 1995. This area is thought to be that of the 'polis' or city referred to in *The Odyssey*. A good water supply, and part of a Cyclopean defensive wall 31.5m long, were first discovered by Heurtley in 1937. In 1995 two gates through this wall were identified by the archaeological team from Ioannina. Quantities of pottery from the Mycenaean Era of Odysseus have been found here, but considerable damage was caused when the area was used as a burial place in later Hellenistic and Classical periods.

There are no remains from these ancient times to be seen on the ground in present day Stavros. However, to follow the next chapters 10 to 16, Stavros makes a good base for study and walks in North Ithaca, as well as for present day accommodation. There are also several small displays and museums to be seen.

First look at the displays in the small park opposite the large church of Agios Sotiras in the main square. Then look around the Museum of the Sea and the exhibition 'Throwing Light on Homeric Ithaca'.

Nobody can be sure of the route taken by Odysseus on his way back from Troy. Homer, our most reliable source, was very unclear about it. However theories abound. Here in the main square of Stavros there is a 3D map which represents one theory of the route taken by Odysseus on his return to Ithaca.

Also in this square, under a small shelter, is a model showing how the Palace of Odysseus might have looked at Agios Athanasios / School of Homer. The model was made by Bruno Mazzati, an Italian architect who lives in the north of Ithaca during the summer months, following discussions with the archaeologist Litsa Kontorli-Papadopoulou.

There is also a bronze bust of Odysseus with the words ΕΥΧΗΝ ΟΔΥΣΣΕΙ (an offering to Odysseus) written on its base. For the significance of this quotation see Chapter 12, page 90.

Two small museums are located immediately after the right-hand fork from the north of Stavros signed to Frikes and Kioni. They are free to enter but, if you can, please make a donation to support their good work.

The 'Museum of the Sea 1200–800 BC'. This dating covers the period from Odysseus up to Homer, and it is a fascinating exploration of the nautical world at that time. The museum was set up and is administered by Bruno Mazzati. It has many details of ships in the years 1200–800 BC, including a large model of a ship such as Odysseus and Telemachus might have used. It also has details of the main northern shipping route from the Eastern Mediterranean to Western Europe at that time. This route passed on either side of Ithaca (both between Ithaca and Lefkas and up the Ithaca Channel between Ithaca and Kefalonia) and then on up to Corfu, and across the Straits of Otranto to Sicily and the heel of Italy.

The exhibition 'Throwing Light on Homeric Ithaca'. This small museum is almost opposite the Museum of the Sea on the same road. It is a permanent display of an exhibition first shown by Dimitris L Paizis-Danias in 2013. It was the result of many years of meticulous research by a retired sea captain from Ithaca, and it gives detailed explanations of the relationship of Homer's ancient story to the island of Ithaca.

Sylvia Benton

11

Sylvia Benton and Polis Bay

See map no.6, page 19

From the main square of Stavros, in front of the large church of Agios Sotiras, make your way down to Polis Bay along 1.2km of winding road with many hairpin bends. If you have a vehicle it is really easier to drive this bit of road. When you arrive at Polis Bay you can drive around the back of the kantina (an elementary café in a caravan allowed on a beach) past a tiny ruined church and a desalination plant on your right-hand side, to park under the trees planted behind the main long beach.

These days Polis Bay is a rural and unassuming place, yet this wasn't always the case. Its unusual name, 'Polis', indicates that a city once existed in this area. At the time of Odysseus the city is thought to have stood on the western slopes of the town now called Stavros.

Down at Polis Bay a sign gives some information about Sylvia Benton. A map shows the position of 'Loïzos' Cave', which she excavated in the 1930s. The cave was partially destroyed in Classical times and the disastrous earthquake of 1953 finished it off. If you swim out in the harbour at Polis Bay you can see the scarring in the rocks left when this cave finally collapsed. It is on the far side of the bay from the kantina, about halfway between the beach and the point of the headland. In this land of earthquakes and changing sea levels, caves near the sea are particularly vulnerable. They come and go, reveal themselves or collapse, with each of the many earthquakes suffered there.

Benton is a largely unsung heroine of Ithaca. Wild and remote places beckoned her, and Ithaca held a particular pull. Some of her most important work was carried out at Polis Bay where, every evening after work, she would swim across the bay and back again. Her swimming, I have been told by those who knew her, showed more strength than style, but she was always athletic. At Cambridge, where she read Classics before the First World War, she played hockey and tennis for her college and university teams. Benton was a bluestocking. She shared her classical interests with her father, who was Chief Judge in the Punjab where she was born in Lahore in 1887. In the late 1920s she studied archaeology at the British School at Athens before reading for a Diploma in Classical Archaeology at Oxford. The title of her B. Litt. dissertation was 'The Barony of Odysseus'. In the early 1930s she was the obvious choice to assist in the excavations on Ithaca under the direction of William Heurtley from the British School at Athens.

Benton excavated Loïzos' Cave in Polis Bay but, as its name suggests, she was not the first to investigate either the cave or the area. Back in the 1860s a local landowner, Dr Dimitris Loïzos, excavated 200 ancient graves on the land adjacent to Polis Bay. Loïzos kept no record of his finds, either in the graves or the nearby cave, and he had a reason for this. He took most of his treasure to Paris where he disposed of it and lived the rest of his life in great luxury. We also know that Loïzos was by no means the only person who looted ancient artefacts from Ithaca. An enormous number of finds were removed in the early years of the 19th century, especially after the British took over the Ionian Islands from the French in 1807. A local Ithacan sea captain and historian, Dimitris Païzis-Danias, recently explained how the Corsican Captain A Guiterra, Commander of the Ionian Islands from 1811 to 1814, became very busy excavating the ancient sites. He made a huge collection of finds, which he later sold in Italy for more than £6,000, a very large sum at the time. Finds taken from Ithaca can be found in museums all over the world, in the Archaeological Museum in Athens, the British Museum and the Society of Antiquaries in London, the Metropolitan Museum in New York, and the Archaeological Museum in Brooklyn, as well as museums in Paris in France, Munich in Germany and Neuchâtel in Switzerland.

The German archaeologist Heinrich Schliemann made brief visits to Ithaca both in 1868 and in 1870 before he went on to excavate at Troy and Mycenae. The record of his visits, neither of which lasted more than 10 days, are now on the internet, but they are written in German. Schliemann reported that he bought some Egyptian scarabs, some coins, and a small statue of the goddess Athena from Dr Loïzos. He made a search for the Palace of Odysseus, not at Agios Athanasios / School of Homer but at a highly fortified site at Alalkomenai that stands above the isthmus that connects the northern and southern parts of the island, see Chapter 17. Research in this area, particularly on the col below the peak, showed that the site was important in the immediate post-Mycenaean period. Although it may have been used earlier as a garrison, its principal use was during the Dark Ages: i.e. after the time of Odysseus but before that of Homer.

Schliemann was a gold-digger, but he didn't find much on Ithaca. As he left for Troy he remarked that the island of Ithaca had been well and truly ransacked by those who came before him. Constantine Cavafy's famous poem Ithaca, written at the end of the 19th century, reflected Schliemann's views when he suggested the traveller should not expect Ithaca to make him rich:

Ithaca gave you the marvellous journey.
Without her you would not have set out.
She has nothing left to give you now.

However between 1932 and 1937 the archaeological team from the British School at Athens under William Heurtley and Sylvia Benton made extensive and careful research and excavations on several sites in north Ithaca. Their finds were carefully photographed and recorded and stored in the two museums they set up on the island. The collapse of Loïzos' Cave in Classical times turned out to be a blessing in disguise. Without it Dr. Loïzos would have taken everything, but the collapse preserved both the stratification of the earth, which archaeologists use to date their finds, and some of the objects inside the cave.

Sylvia Benton, top right, excavating the cave at Polis Bay

In the 1930s Benton brought a pump by boat from Patras on the mainland over to Ithaca and, by pumping the seawater out from Loïzos' Cave she managed to dig down through several strata below the apparent floor, where she found many objects that Loïzos had missed. She discovered that this cave had been used as a place of worship since 3000 BC, and probably for much longer, as she excavated votive offerings to the chthonic gods of the underworld from way before the time of Odysseus. Later, she believed, the cave was used for the hero-worship of Odysseus himself. Confirmation of this is found in a small triangular-shaped sherd of pottery Benton discovered there. It sits, with little explanation, on a shelf in the one-room Archaeological Collection of Stavros.

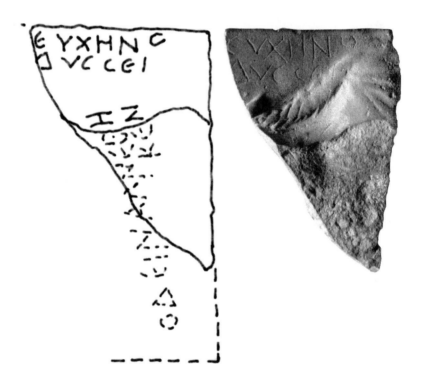

A sherd from a ceramic mask from the 2nd century BC
found in Loizos' Cave

12

The Archaeological Collection of Stavros

See map no.6, page 19

Visit the Archaeological Collection of Stavros (Αρχαιολογική Συλλογή Σταυρά). This small museum is currently open from 8.30am to 4pm (last entrance 3.45pm). The cost is 3€, or 2€ for concessions. It is closed on Tuesdays.

The Archaeological Collection of Stavros is at Pelikata to the north of Stavros very close to our Viewing Point on the Hill of Hermes. This little museum, which was set up by the archaeologist Sylvia Benton in the 1930s, is a treasure trove of ancient objects found in north Ithaca. They date from before and over the time of Odysseus, up to and including finds from the Roman rule of Ithaca ending in 396 AD. The collection includes some things that relate directly to Homer's story, for instance the remains of several tripod-lebetes such as those that Odysseus brought back from Phaeacia and hid in the Cave of the Nymphs. It also displays a small sherd of pottery from the 2nd century BC inscribed with the message EYXHN ΟΔΥΣΣΕΙ, 'An offering to Odysseus'. This sherd, and the tripods, were discovered by Benton in the cave down near Polis Bay known as Loïzos' Cave.

If you are walking from Stavros it is more pleasant to take the quieter route along the back streets rather than walk along the road with the cars. In addition you will avoid the perennial problem of parking near the museum. This is an easy walk along small quiet roads. The distance is about a kilometre and it will take approximately 18 minutes in each direction.

Set off from the centre of Stavros along the road marked to Platreithias. If you are on foot ignore the road sign (straight on) marked 'Archaeological Museum', and turn immediately right up the smaller road marked 'Iriana Village'. At the junction where the tarmac deteriorates follow the road up the hill to the left, again marked 'Iriana'. After about 100m the road, which is marked by a blue and white Avenza sign, turns into a dirt footpath across a field until it rejoins another tarmac road. This will bring you on to the main Stavros to Platreithias road just before the turn-off to the right to the Archaeological Museum. Take a right turn up this road, and follow it around to the left. After a few houses you will find the Archaeological Collection of Stavros on your right-hand side.

To reach the museum by car or scooter take the same left-hand fork at the northern end of Stavros signed to Platreithias. Continue along this road for about 1km until you find a sign to your right saying Archaeological Museum. Take this turn up a steep and narrow road. If there is room for you to park at the point where this road turns to the left, I suggest you do so. From there you can walk to the left until, after a few houses, you find the museum on your right-hand side.

In the museum you will see the small sherd of pottery illustrated on page 88. It doesn't look much. There is no explanation in English and you could easily miss it. But amongst fragments from around a hundred clay female masks from the 2nd century BC Benton found this one with the words ΕΥΧΗΝ ΟΔΥΣΣΕΙ (an offering to Odysseus) scratched into it. Two letters which can be seen on the edge 'H*N' probably belong to the word 'ΑΝΕΘΗΚΕΝ' (dedicated) before which might have been the name of the person making the dedication.

It is hard to read the lettering on the little piece of broken pottery, but a helpful photograph and a drawing at a larger scale stand beside it. It is rather overshadowed on its museum shelf by a flashy pair of tasselled gold earrings and a large gold ring. These were recently found up at the Agios Athanasios site, but they date from the later Hellenistic Period.

In a showcase at the far end of the room are some other finds that relate directly to Homer's story of Odysseus. Here the visitor can see the remains of the 12 bronze tripod-lebetes (lebetes is the plural of lebes) found by Benton in Loïzos' Cave. A tripod-lebes was originally a cauldron or cooking pot where the cauldron (the lebes) was supported over a fire on three legs (the tripod). Simpler versions were made of earthenware but the grander tripods, like these, were made of bronze. A little picture adjacent to the showcase shows a reconstructed whole bronze tripod-lebes. It is a somewhat ungainly object with metre long legs supporting a wide, shallow cauldron. On each side of the cauldron's rim stand two large circular handles, placed vertically and topped with lively bronze statuettes of horses or goats.

A strange thing relates to the number of tripods found. Sylvia Benton found the remains of 12, but a 13th had been found by Loïzos. When she first arrived in Ithaca Benton interviewed two local men. One had worked for Loïzos on his excavations, the other had been host to Schliemann in Vathi. Both men independently told her that Loïzos had found a complete tripod-lebes in the cave at Polis Bay but that later, when the authorities got wind of it, he melted it down! There is nothing in the small museum at Stavros to explain the extraordinary Homeric significance of the fact that 13 of these objects were found at Loïzos' Cave in Polis Bay. To understand this we have to go back to Homer's story.

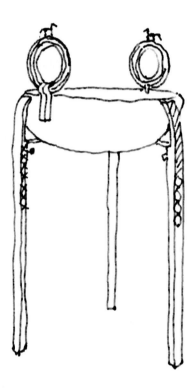

According to Homer, when he was nearing the end of his 10-year journey home from Troy, Odysseus managed to struggle ashore in Phaeacia, thought to be modern Corfu. By this time he had lost all his ships and all his men. The generous king and queen of the Phaeacians invited him to join them in a banquet they were holding. After Odysseus revealed his identity they, and their guests, gave him the gifts that he later hid in the Cave of the Nymphs. In addition to *gold and sumptuous clothes* the king and queen gave Odysseus a 'large tripod and a cauldron'. The king also arranged for each of the 12 noblemen present at the banquet to do the same:

"The clothing, gold ornaments and other presents that our counsellors brought here are already packed for our guest in a polished strong-box. I now suggest that in addition we each give him a large tripod and a cauldron.

(13: 11-13)

This made 13 tripod-lebetes in all.

You might wonder if the remains of 13 bronze tripod-lebetes in the museum in north Ithaca could actually be fragments of those brought back to Ithaca by Odysseus on his return after 20 years. Unfortunately the dating indicates that this is not so, as the tripods found in the cave at Polis Bay date from the Dark Ages: i.e. between the time of Odysseus (during the Palace Civilisation of the Mycenaeans) but before the time of Homer (and the extraordinary flowering of Classical Greece). For this reason many experienced Homerists have made a different suggestion. They believe that Homer himself visited Ithaca to check the details of a pre-existing story, which had been passed down orally for generations, before his epic poem was recorded in writing. They suggest that Homer based his story of a gift of 13 tripods on the fact that he himself saw 13 when he made a visit to Ithaca.

Coins weren't yet invented in the days of Odysseus and bronze tripods were valuable. They could be given as gifts or used as barter for trade. In *The Iliad* an 'ordinary' bronze tripod had the same value as an ox, but a 'fine' one was described as a '12-ox tripod'. The Greeks sometimes used grand ones, like those found on Ithaca, as centrepieces at their feasts. They also gave them as prizes in their athletic games. Behind the car parking area at Polis Bay there is a patch of wide flat land. A notice says that camping and campervans are prohibited there from 1st July to 31st August. This land, inland from the long beach, is thought by archaeologists to be the site of the pre-Olympic Odyssean Games.

Athletic competitions were a favourite male pastime in those ancient days. In *The Iliad* Homer records the hero Achilles organising competitive games at Troy and, in *The Odyssey*, he tells how King Alcinous of the Phaeacians organised racing, wrestling, chariot racing, discus throwing and boxing contests in honour of his guest Odysseus. A prize given for a supreme athletic feat at such games could be a large bronze tripod-lebes. Benton investigated the link between these tripods and the athletic games of ancient times. Fragments of around 200 grand bronze tripods were discovered in Olympia on the nearby mainland, where the Olympic Games were first held in 776 BC. Around 200 grand bronze tripods were also found at Delphi, site of the famous Shrine of the Oracle. And 23 were found at the Idaean Cave on Mount Ida in Crete, where the legend says the god Zeus was born. Next on the list comes Ithaca, where 13 bronze tripod-lebetes were discovered. Ithaca looks like an anomaly on Benton's list as it has always been a small and relatively impoverished island, but she felt that this pointed to a very important shrine on Ithaca in ancient times – at Loïzos' Cave in Polis Bay – situated directly on the main shipping route to Italy and the West.

In the 2nd century BC, a tablet was sent by the people of Ithaca to the people of Magnesia in faraway Asia Minor. It invited them to their athletic games, which they called the Odysseia. This tablet can be seen in the Museen zu Berlin. The name of the Ithacan Games, Odysseia, clearly links them to the island's ancient hero, Odysseus. Interestingly the Odysseia long pre-date the better-known Olympic Games. Benton believed that these games were performed in the flattish valley behind the long beach at Polis Bay.

During the Second World War, back in London, Benton worked for the Naval Hydrography department to produce a *Gazeteer of Greece* and a *Glossary of Modern Greek*. She then worked in the 'uncommon languages' section of the Postal Censorship Department, as well as fire-fighting by night. By 1947 she was back in Ithaca where she worked principally on the post-war restoration of the museums in Vathi and Stavros. She was not on the island at the time of the terrible earthquake in 1953, but she managed to hitch a lift back right away on a Royal Navy destroyer carrying relief supplies. Although she was, by this time, in her late sixties she couldn't bring herself to use the ladder to get into the sea for a swim, but insisted in diving from the deck!

Benton found the earthquake had badly damaged the Vathi Museum and much of its contents, although Stavros fared slightly better. Many of the finds were taken to Patras and Athens for conservation and, along with the islanders, she had a hard fight to get them back. The repair and reconstruction of the two museums on Ithaca took many years and, in her eighties in the mid-1970s, Benton was still bringing groups of students from the British School at Athens to show them around the archaeological sites of Ithaca.

If you have not yet been to the Viewing Point on the Hill of Hermes (see Chapter 9, page 73) you might like to walk along there now. It is 300m past the Archaeological Collection of Stavros along the same road.

"Eumaeus," said Odysseus, taking the swineherd by the arm, "this must surely be Odysseus' palace: it would be easy to pick it out at a glance from any number of houses. There are buildings beyond buildings; the courtyard wall with its coping is a fine piece of work and those folding doors are true defences.
No one could storm it."

The Odyssey, Book 17: 262-267

13

From Polis Bay to the Palace of Odysseus at Agios Athanasios / School of Homer

See map no.6, page 19

This walk is relatively easy and mostly along dirt tracks or roads. Without diversions the distance is 3km and, at moderate speed, it will take an hour going up and 50 minutes to return.

There are two routes marked on the Topo map from Polis Bay to the site of Odysseus' Palace at Agios Athanasios / School of Homer. There is a dirt road marked in yellow and, to the west of it, a path marked as a dotted black line. The path to the west, higher up the hill, may well be an original Homeric path as it is a very direct route between Loizos Cave and the palace site. However don't try to take this path, which does not feature on the Avenza map. As of summer 2021 only the southern section of this higher path is passable and the northern section is clear only at its northern end. Several trees have fallen across it, and it has an impassable and potentially treacherous area midway. If you try to take this route you may damage your legs or get lost, or both.

I advise you to take the main routes shown on the Topo, the Avenza, and my own map. First walk westwards along the length of the long beach at Polis Bay, passing the site of the Odyssean Games on your right. At the far end of the beach you will meet a barbed wire fence. Don't be dismayed as, if you walk a few steps to the right, you can skirt around the end of it. At this point there is no sign of a path but, higher up, you will see another fence continuing up the hill. Walk straight ahead up the hill, through a field of thistles and olives, and then keep to the right of this fence (don't take the path to the left of the fence). This path will lead you directly onto a well-defined dirt track. Turn to the right along this track.

'Loizos' Cave' once stood by the sea to the south of this area. The cave, excavated by Benton in the 1930s, has since totally collapsed in the major earthquake of 1953. Also in this area there is an unexcavated Mycenaean site called Trilagkata (marked Trelagkada and Τρελάγκαδα on the Topo map). Both Benton, and subsequently Kontorli-Papadopoulou made trial pits in this area. From their finds, they believed that a Mycenaean fishing village once stood here.

Keep walking to the north along this dirt track, onwards and upwards, ignoring all incoming paths. After about 1km a footpath from Stavros, which Avenza has marked, crosses the track, but carry straight on. Ignore another track coming in from the left, which leads to the locked church of Panagia. The road is in better condition here. It is concreted and marked ΟΔΟΣ ΙΩΑΚΕΙΜ ΜΕΤΑΛΟΓΕΝΝΗ. Continue along this road, past a few houses until, at about 1.9km from the start, you arrive on the tarmacked Stavros to Platreithias road opposite a sign on a wall saying ΡΟΜΑΝΤΣΑ (romance!). Turn to the left along this road then, where the road is signed Εξωγή (Exoghi) and School of Homer, turn left; then right at a hairpin bend onto the main access road to the Palace of Odysseus marked Archaeological Site Agios Athanasios / School of Homer. At 3km from the start of your walk you will reach the lower end of the site of the Palace of Odysseus on the left-hand side.

To reach the upper end of the fenced archaeological site, where the next walk begins, take the upper part of the footpath marked as 15 on map No.7. Walk past the EU rest stop on the left-hand side to the upper gate on your right. The upper gate is 250m from the parking place at the lower end of the site.

13a

If you have not already visited the Archaeological Collection of Stavros (see Chapter 12, page 89) make a small diversion to do this when you join the Stavros to Platreithias road at the sign saying ΡΟΜΑΝΤΣΑ. Cross over the road and, almost opposite, follow a brown sign saying 'Archaeological Museum' in yellow (the Greek) and white (the English). Walk up a steep slope then follow the road as it turns at 90° to the left. Continue past a few houses on the right-hand side until you find the museum.

If you haven't been to the Viewing Point (see page 75) you can also continue on this road along the 'Hill of Hermes' until you meet a T junction. To re-join the original itinerary follow the road downhill to the left. Then turn right onto the Stavros/Platreithias road a short distance before the left turn towards Exoghi.

Elevation and isometric reconstruction of the megaron (main hall) of the Palace of Odysseus at Agios Athanasios / School of Homer

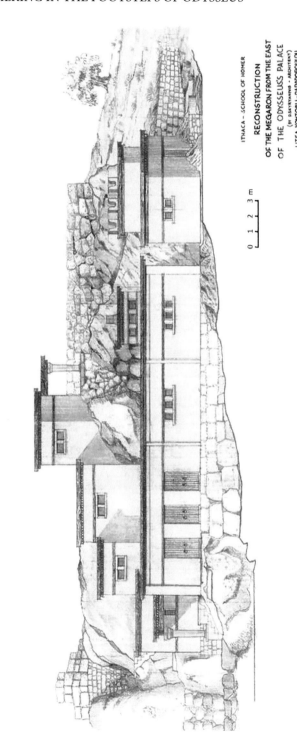

ITHACA - SCHOOL OF HOMER

RECONSTRUCTION
OF THE MEGARON FROM THE EAST
OF THE ODYSSEUS'S PALACE
(BY S.SKITRIKINIS - ARCHITECT)
LITSA KONTORLI-PAPADOPOULOU
ASSOC. PROF. OF PREHIST. ARCHAEOLOGY

0 1 2 3 m

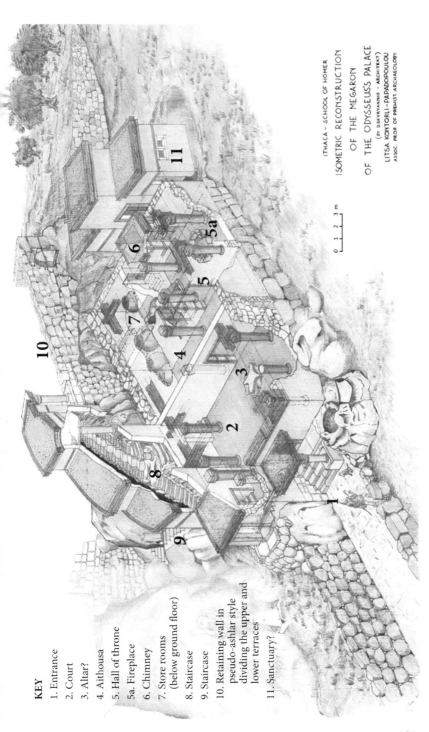

KEY

1. Entrance
2. Court
3. Altar?
4. Aithousa
5. Hall of throne
5a. Fireplace
6. Chimney
7. Store rooms (below ground floor)
8. Staircase
9. Staircase
10. Retaining wall in pseudo-ashlar style dividing the upper and lower terraces
11. Sanctuary?

ITHACA – SCHOOL OF HOMER
ISOMETRIC RECONSTRUCTION
OF THE MEGARON
OF THE ODYSSEUS'S PALACE
(BY D.SKYRYANNIS – ARCHITEKT)
LITSA KONTORLI-PAPADOPOULOU
ASSOC. PROF. OF PREHIST. ARCHAEOLOGY

0 1 2 3 m

101

Aerial view of the site

The cliff separating the two levels can be seen across the centre of the photograph.

Photographed with temporary covers over the excavation pits as it was left in 2011.

View of the lower level taken from the upper level

Photographed with temporary covers over the excavation pits as the site was left in 2011.

Survey of the site showing the excavated areas

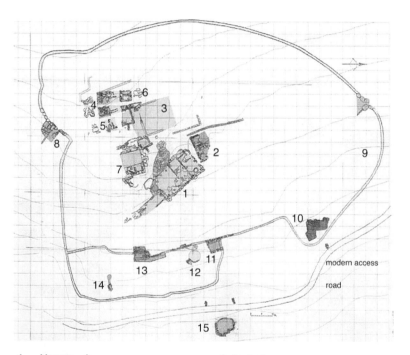

1. Megaron A	9. North Gate
2. Tripartite Temple	10. Burial Monument
3. Megaron B?	11. North east Gate
4. Metallurgical Workshop	12. Tholos?
5. Bathroom	13. East Gate
6. Store Rooms	14. Underground Spring
7. Hellenistic Tower	15. Kykloteres
8. Southwest Gate	

Plan of the megaron

Made for the archaeologist Litsa Kontorli-Papadopoulou
by the architect Dimitris Skirgiannis.

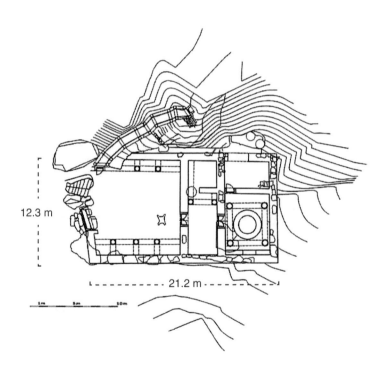

12.3 m

21.2 m

1m   5m   10m

Isometric reconstruction of both levels of the Palace of Odysseus

Made for the archaeologist Litsa Kontorli-Papadopoulou
by the architect Dimitris Skirgiannis.

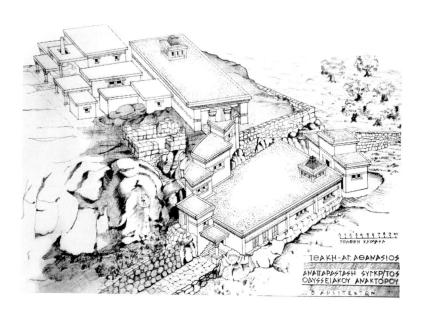

14

The Palace of Odysseus

See map no.7, page 20

Recommended reading:

1. *The Odyssey* Books 17-24 for Homer's story of the tumultuous series of events that followed Odysseus' homecoming.

2. *The Excavation at Agios Athanasios / School of Homer: The Archaeological Evidence for the Palace of Odysseus on Ithaca* by Professor Thanasis J Papadopoulos describes the archaeological work carried out at this site between 1994 and 2011. This is best professional record of the excavation at Agios Athanasios currently available in English. This can be obtained in ebook form through the following link: www.amazon.co.uk/dp/B09QF67T3J. This account originally formed part of a larger paper *'Mycenaean citadels of Western Greece: architecture, purpose and their intricate role in the local communities and their relations with the West'*. It was presented by Thanasis Papadopoulos at a conference *'ΕΣΠΕΡΟΣ/ HESPEROS, the Aegean seen from the West'* held in Ioannina in May 2016. The proceedings from the conference were published in 2017 by Peeters publishers in Belgium. With their permission I have extracted the portion dealing with the site in Ithaca and, in collaboration with Professor Papadopoulos, I have added an introduction and a few explanations to

clarify the archaeological terminology to help non-specialists in this field. Many of the Late Bronze Age finds at this site are illustrated in this small publication.

3. My book *Odysseus' Island* Chapter 15 p.287 onwards, and my notes 15-23 pp.328-331, for my analysis and understanding of the situation at the palace site.

4. *The Heroon of Odysseus at Ithaca. Reconsidered* by Thanasis J Papadopoulos describing the archaeological work at this site will be made available online by the University of Ioannina.

The site of the Palace of Odysseus is fenced. It has two gates, which are currently not locked. I describe the site from entry by the upper gate, but this walk can be reversed.

It is well worth going with a guide on this walk. If they have time either Ester van Zuylen of Island Walks 00 30 6944 990458 ester@islandwalks. com or Spiros Couvaras 00 30 697 2031453 s.covaras@gmail.com will give you a very good explanation of the site.

The site of the Palace of Odysseus now carries the cumbersome name of Agios Athanasios / School of Homer. Neither name is helpful. Agios Athanasios (St Athanasios) is the dedication of the Greek Orthodox church built on the site in the 17th century AD, which now lies in ruins at the upper level of the site. The name School of Homer is equally misleading. As far as we know the poet Homer never either attended or taught at a school in the north of Ithaca. He is thought to have come from the farthest part of the Greek world, either from the island of Chios or from the adjacent mainland that is now part of Turkey. In the early 19th century the Homerist

William Gell visited the site at Agios Athanasios and an old priest showed him around. He told Gell that the site had been the capital of the island under Roman rule, for 600 years up to 396 AD, and this was probably true. The priest didn't tell Gell that the site had also been in use long before the time of the Romans, in fact also during the time of Odysseus. Possibly he didn't know this himself. The priest called the site the School of Homer (a name quite often used for ancient sites in Greece) and the name stuck.

In 1932, when Heurtley and Benton from the British School at Athens started their archaeological work in Ithaca, they made preliminary investigations at Aetos and Alalkomenai as well as several Mycenaean sites in north Ithaca: at Loïzos' Cave, in Stavros itself, at Pelikata, at Trilagkada, and at Agios Athanasios / School of Homer. Their investigations led them to believe that Odysseus' Palace would not be found on the rocky outcrop of Alalkomenai on the isthmus between the southern and northern parts of the island. They went on to excavate more thoroughly at Loïzos' Cave and at Pelikata. But when their work was interrupted by the Second World War, they had not finally agreed between themselves whether Pelikata (around our viewing spot on the Hill of Hermes) or Agios Athanasios was the true site of Odysseus' Palace. Both had freshwater wells and both had remains and fortifications from the Mycenaean Period.

The Second World War was followed by the Greek Civil War then, in 1953, the Ionian Islands suffered a devastating earthquake centred on Kefalonia and Ithaca. Mass emigration from these islands followed. It was not until 1994 that archaeologists from Ioannina University in north-western Greece were able to continue the work of Heutley and Benton. Litsa Kontorli-Papadopoulou and her small team worked for a month at a time, which was all they could afford, over a period of seven years before finally, in August 2010, she made her dramatic announcement at a *Conference of the Odyssey* in Vathi. The archaeologists had identified a *megaron*, or great hall, placed within a palace complex, from the time of Odysseus, at Agios Athanasios / School of Homer. The *megaron* lay within defensive walls from the Mycenaean era of Odysseus. It corresponded in type, construction and dimensions both with other *megara* from that period found at Mycenae, Tiryns and Pylos, and with the descriptions given by Homer in his epic poem. Kontorli-Papadopoulou explained that the site, which overlooks the fertile plain of north Ithaca, has a plentiful supply of fresh water, and easy access to three alternative harbours for travel, trade and, if necessary, to escape from pirates. She confirmed the site was a *'powerful and affluent political centre and area for worship'* and that it was in continuous use between 1500 and 300 BC; thus before, during, and after the time of both Odysseus and of Homer.

Unfortunately ongoing habitation on the site made archaeological analysis difficult. Later rebuilding on the same area had disturbed the stratification and concealed many of the remains from the time of Odysseus. Stones were used and re-used, and new foundations and graves were dug down through areas where previous buildings stood. Further confusion was caused by the huge and very obvious stones from the base of the ruined 17th-century AD church of Agios Athanasios, which date from a later period well after the time of Odysseus. However, as the excavation progressed Litsa Kontorli-Papadopoulou and Thanasis Papadopoulos realised that their discoveries corresponded precisely with descriptions given in Homer's epic poem *The Odyssey*. They became increasingly certain that they were excavating the site of the Palace of Odysseus described by Homer. When, in 2010, they announced their findings, it should have been a high point for their work, but instead it was the last year of their excavation on Ithaca. Disaster struck again. The world financial crash of 2008 hit Greece badly. What scant money there was for excavation was diverted elsewhere and then, in 2015,

Litsa Kontorli-Papadopoulou died suddenly of a stroke.

The partly-excavated site at Agios Athanasios / School of Homer was left as it was when work stopped in 2010. Kontorli-Papadopoulou had erected temporary covers to protect the excavation pits. You can see these in the aerial views of the site, and of the *megaron* (main hall) taken in 2011, see pages 102-103. Unfortunately, since her death, her work has not been continued or even maintained. The site was left unfenced. Weeds, small shrubs and even trees grew up amongst the ruins. The covers over the open excavation pits began to rot and, when a devastating cyclone hit the island in September 2020, they were finally destroyed. At the time of writing the remnants of the covers have been burned and the excavation pits are still open. Huge rainstorms in the autumn of 2021 flooded the pits. As I write, in December 2021 it is exposed, dangerous and vulnerable. There is no explanation on the site to help visitors. Please take great care both of yourselves and of the site, cause no damage and take nothing.

Agios Athanasios / School of Homer is a perfect site for the palace of a Mycenaean king. The archaeological site has an area of 23 hectares on high ground to give safety from attack by pirates. It is surrounded by defensive walls from the Mycenaean era, which have now been located. It overlooks the fertile plain of north Ithaca, where olives, vines and fruit trees grow to this day. Three harbours are easily accessible from this site – Polis Bay to the south, Afales Bay to the north, and Frikes (Rheithron) Bay to the east. These harbours not only offered means of escape, but access to three different seas for travel and trade. The ever-flowing wells in the area provided plentiful supplies of fresh water.

As you enter the archaeological site at the upper level the building most easily seen today is the ruined 17th-century church of Agios Athanasios and adjacent ruined cottages, but this was not the case in Odysseus' time. At the base of the walls of the church you will see huge stone blocks from an earlier building. These very obvious blocks, which date from a thousand years after the time of Odysseus around the 3rd century BC have, in the past, led many archaeologists to assume that this site was not from the Mycenaean era of Odysseus. But further careful work by Kontorli-Papadopoulou and her team found the remains of earlier defensive walls, buildings and a well from his time. At the upper level they discovered many foundations that they believe to be women's rooms, along with a women's hall. Dimitris Skirgiannis' drawings are based on accurate measurements of the foundations found on the site and the archaeologists' knowledge of building types of that era.

The ruined church of Agios Athanassios

A fascinating find at this upper level was a bath from the time of Odysseus.

THE PALACE OF ODYSSEUS

There are many descriptions in *The Iliad* and *The Odyssey* of Homer's cast bathing in just such a bath. I will give one example. Homer tells how, on his visit to Pylos, Telemachus was bathed by King Nestor's daughter Polycaste:

'The beautiful Polycaste, King Nestor's youngest daughter, now bathed Telemachus. When she had bathed him and rubbed him with olive oil, she gave him a tunic and arranged a fine cloak around his shoulders, so he stepped from the bath looking like an immortal god.'

(3: 464-469)

If you visit the Palace of Nestor at Epano Englianos 11 miles to the north of the modern city of Pylos, you will see a bath from the Mycenaean era of Nestor restored and centrally displayed in the main hall. A similar (but less damaged) bath was discovered here at Agios Athanasios / School of Homer in north Ithaca. This one has yet to be restored and is not yet on display.

The Palace of Nestor at Pylos is the best-preserved Mycenaean palace in Greece. Careful excavation, funded by the University of Cincinnati, continues to this day. In 2016 a handsome new metal roof and raised viewing galleries were completed over the main hall. The visitor can look down from suspended walkways to view the remains of the walls, now mostly less than a metre high. The layout of the main hall and its surrounding anterooms can clearly be seen. The Mycenaean bath, restored from fragments, stands centrally. It is a model of how an archaeological site can be both preserved and displayed.

At the upper level of the Palace of Odysseus the archaeologists found a metallurgy workshop from the Mycenaean era where a bronze-casting stone can still clearly be seen. It was recognised as such by Professor Papademetriou of the National Technical University in Athens. Many little metal objects from the Late Bronze Age, for instance bronze pins, nails, fishhooks and lamps, were found nearby.

A bronze-casting stone from the Mycenaean era of Odysseus

In *The Odyssey* Books 22-24 Homer told a great story, but did he imagine that these dramatic events took place on this very hillside in Ithaca? To answer this question we can compare his descriptions with details of the remains found by archaeologists on this site.

A scramble around to the east of the Hellenistic Tower, at the base of the ruined church of Agios Athanasios, will reveal a well-preserved, steep and narrow staircase, cut into the bedrock of the cliff. It is one of three discovered running between the two levels.

Over and over Homer refers to these two levels with their interconnecting stairs. In his story Penelope's room, and those of her entourage, lay at the top of a steep staircase, while the main drama was played out in the main hall, or *megaron*, on the lower level. I will give two examples:

In her room upstairs Penelope...took in the words of his stirring ballad and came down from her quarters by the steep staircase.

(1: 329-331)

She left her room and made her way downstairs, a prey to indecision.

(23: 84)

A steep and narrow staircase between the two levels

At the base of the cliff are the remains of the *megaron*, or main hall. Here, if the archaeologists from Ioannina are correct, Homer envisaged Odysseus' eventual reunion with Penelope and his great battle with the suitors (*The Odyssey* Books 18 to 21 inclusive). He told the touching story of Odysseus' meeting with his old hunting dog Argos at the entrance porch (17: 290-327), of his challenging encounter with Irus, a genuine beggar (18: 1-110),

115

of how Penelope devised a test to see who could string her husband's old bow and shoot an arrow through 12 axe heads (19: 572-586 and 21: 1-423) and how, to the suitors' disgust, only Odysseus (still disguised as a beggar) won the contest. He told how the old servant woman Eurycleia discovered true Odysseus' identity when she washed his legs and saw the scars from an incident where, as a young man, he was tusked by a wild boar (19: 349-507). In Book 22, Homer described in gruesome detail how Odysseus and his small team of three went on to kill every one of Penelope's suitors until they lay in heaps:

> '...like fish that the fishermen have dragged out of the grey surf in the meshes of their net on to a curving beach, to lie in masses on the sand longing for the salt water, till the bright sun ends their lives.'
>
> (22: 382-386)

And finally Odysseus:

> ... 'stood among the corpses of the dead, splattered with blood and gore, like a lion when he comes from feeding on some farmer's bullock, with the blood dripping from his breast and jaws on either side, a fearsome spectacle.'
>
> (22: 400-404)

Homer told how Odysseus followed up on the slaughter by organising the hanging of the 'disloyal' maidservants who had slept with the suitors in his absence (22: 430-473) and of his final reconciliation when Penelope finally recognises Odysseus for himself. The scene (see The Odyssey, Book 23: 1-296) took place adjacent to a fireplace surrounded by columns just as can be seen in the third room of the main hall.

This could have been the very place where Homer envisaged the touching reunion between Odysseus and Penelope.

The hearth

In their interpretation of the archaeological remains at this site Kontorli-Papadopoulou and her team had a great advantage over Heurtley and Benton. Since the 1930s other Mycenaean sites, with similarly designed palace halls and wells, have been professionally dated to the time of Odysseus. Archaeologists are now able to compare the layout of this hall with that of known Mycenaean halls at Mycenae, Tiryns and Pylos. An account of these comparisons is made by Thanasis Papadopoulos in his paper 'Mycenaean citadels of Western Greece: architecture, purpose and their intricate role in the local communities and their relations with the West' published by Peeters publishers in Belgium in a compendium titled 'ΕΣΠΕΡΟΣ/ HESPEROS, the Aegean seen from the West' (see the recommended reading at the head of this chapter, p.107).

Homer envisaged Odysseus (who was still in disguise) and Eumaeus approaching the palace from the south-east at this lower level:

'Eumaeus,' said Odysseus, taking the swineherd by the arm, 'this must surely be Odysseus' palace: it would be easy to pick it out at a glance from any number of houses. There are buildings beyond buildings; the courtyard wall with its coping is a fine piece of work and those folding doors are true defences. No one could storm it.'

(17: 262-267)

This description fits the architect Dimitris Skirgiannis' isometric drawings of the palace made for the archaeologists, see page 106, where *'buildings beyond buildings'* on two levels can clearly be seen.

On Skirgiannis' plan of the *megaron* at the head of this chapter, p105, you will see the overall dimensions of the hall are 22.20m x 12.30m. It is not big, but Odysseus was known for his wits, not his wealth. The hall is divided into three main sections. In the open court of the *megaron*, a relief of the rough shape of an 'ox-hide ingot' of 'talanton' can be seen cut into the bedrock.

Odysseus lived in the Late Bronze Age. Bronze for the armour and weapons used in the Trojan War was made from approximately 90% copper and 10% tin. This shape, reminiscent of the stretched hide of an ox, was that of the copper ingots used for making bronze. The concave sides and protruding corners of the ingots made them easy to carry and pack for transport. In this time before coinage the ingot formed a stable means of trade. Its shape may have been a reminder of previous animal transactions. In Papadopoulos' paper he surmises that the ox-hide shape carved into the bedrock at Agios Athanasios might have been used as an altar for the sacrifice of animals to the gods. In the nearby *kykloteres*, or tholos tomb, archaeologists found the bones of oxen, and also of the *bos primigenius*, killed in sacrifice. The *bos primigenius*, or auroch, was a species of wild horned cattle that is now extinct. It was dark in colour and about 6ft or 1.8m tall to the shoulder.

Shape of an 'oxhide ingot or τάλαντον (talanton) cut into the bedrock
Possibly used as an altar

In the second room the circular hole and deep pit that you will see is called a *bothros*. It was probably used for food storage.

Circular bothros (round storage container)

In the third room the archaeologists uncovered the remains of the 3m diameter circular fireplace (see p.117).

Adjacent to the cliff and dug to a lower level, a storeroom from the Mycenaean era was excavated by the archaeologists. Homer describes how Telemachus left the main hall and:

> ...'went down to his father's store-room, a big and lofty chamber stacked with gold and bronze, and with chests full of clothing, and stores of fragrant oil. There too, packed close along the wall, stood jars of mellow vintage wine...'

(2: 337-341)

Along the wall of the store room, adjacent to the cliff, stood a row of old terracotta wine jars such as Skirgiannis has drawn in his isometric reconstruction at the head of this chapter, p101.

The extracts quoted above appear to perfectly fit the ancient words of Homer. There is, however, one passage that is questioned by scholars. The Odyssey Book 16 describes how the suitors saw a ship arriving at Polis Bay from a place that appears to be directly in front of the Palace of Odysseus. After Eumaeus had delivered his message to Penelope that Telemachus was safely back in Ithaca:

> 'To the Suitors the news came as a shock that cast a gloom over their spirits. They streamed out of the hall through the high-walled courtyard, and there in front of the gates they held a meeting. Eurymachus, son of Polybus, was first to speak... He was still speaking when Amphinomus, turning round, caught sight of their ship from where he sat.'

(16: 341-344 and 352-353)

There is no view of Polis Bay from a place directly in front of the megaron at Agios Athanasios. In fact, along modern roads, you need to walk 0.95km from the upper gate at Agios Athanasios to get a good view down into Polis Bay such as Homer describes. There is a well-attested textual variant that eases this problem replacing, in translation, the word for 'just there' with that for 'near'. Back then, when long distances were walked on foot, a distance of less than a kilometer would definitely have been considered 'near', but I leave it to philologists to discuss these points.

Homer was a poet, not a geographer and, given the history of his epic poem - passed down orally for generations, copied out by hand over and over, a definitive version made for the library in Alexandria where it survived several sieges and fires, first printed in Greek in Florence in 1488 AD and then the many translations into English – it is remarkable that so many similarities with the actual island of Ithaca remain.

The archaeologists found a large door opening in the northern wall of the *megaron* leading to a three-roomed building, orientated east-west, immediately adjacent to the *megaron*. The finds discovered there – two large triton shell trumpets, one Minoan lead votive idol of a worshiper, a stone altar-shaped seal, two stone feet and a model column in ivory – all had religious significance. They judged from the position and architecture of the building, and the finds discovered there, that this was probably a religious sanctuary in the Late Bronze Age era of Odysseus.

Walking down from the excavations of the main hall you will come to a hole in the ground at the base of an olive tree. This is a well from the Mycenaean era of Odysseus.

You can climb down its corbelled stone shaft and look into a circular pool of dark water 1.6m in diameter, but please take care.

Kontorli-Papadopoulou commissioned Professor Jost Knauss, a leading German expert on Mycenaean hydraulics, to investigate the complicated underground water system at the Agios Athanasios site. Knauss was able to compare this well with similar well-houses, or spring-chambers, at Mycenae, Tiryns, Agia Eirini on Kea and at the capital of the Hittite Empire at Hattusa before he dated this well to the Mycenaean era c.1300-1200 BC. It lies within the main defensive walls of the palace site, directly below the position of the main hall, where it was present at the time of Odysseus.

A Corbelled Well from the Mycenaean era of Odysseus

It is a good precaution, in case of a siege, to have a well that never dries within the palace walls. In spring this pool is full or possibly overflowing. By the autumn you will look down the circular stone-lined shaft to find the water at a lower level.

THE PALACE OF ODYSSEUS

Dimitris Paizis-Danias in his book *The Archaeological Treasures of Ithaca* quotes Thanasis Papadopoulos as saying "according to the facts as they are presented today… with every scientific reservation, we believe that we stand before the palace structure of Odysseus and Penelope, the only palace of the Homeric epics that has yet to be uncovered."

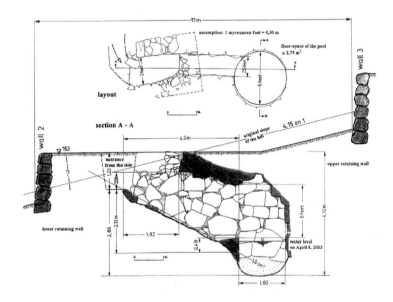

The underground well-house fro the Mycenaean era. Drawing by Prof. J. Knauss.

You can leave the archaeological site through the lower gate below the Mycenaean well.

The girls heard and obeyed. Twenty went off to draw water from the dark waters of the well.

The Odyssey, Book 20: 156-159

15

From Platreithias to the Palace of Odysseus

See map no.7, page 20

Walk from Platreithias up the ancient stepped path to the site of Odysseus' Palace at Agios Athanasios. (See Map No.6 page 18) This is quite a simple uphill walk taking in the Melanhydros (dark water) Springs, and on to the upper entrance to the palace site. Distance: 0.54km. Walking time: 15 minutes.

Go to the Gefuri restaurant in Platreithias and park here if you have come by car or scooter.

Gefuri means 'bridge' in Greek and you will notice that in front of the restaurant the road bridges over a deep gulley. This gulley takes the water down to the sea from the many sweet water springs that surround the site of the Palace of Odysseus. The hillside of the palace site is filled with water. There are several wells and fountains in this area, which flow all year round. In the summer months the gulley by the Gefuri restaurant is dry, but after the winter rains it fills with torrents of water overflowing from the dark Melanhydros Springs near the palace site at Agios Athanasios.

The ancient stepped track going up the hill from the Gefuri restaurant is signed SCHOOL OF HOMER ARCHAEOLOGICAL SITE ΣΧΟΛΗ OMHPOY with an arrow pointing to the footpath. In the summer of 2021 the path was only partially cleared but still passable. When you look at it carefully you can see that the original stone-paved, small-stepped donkey track was at least 2.5m wide. Adjacent to it to the left you will see the watercourse, which runs back down to the Gefuri crossroads.

Path from the Gefuri restaurant up to the Palace of Odysseus

Later you will share the track with one, or sometimes several, black hosepipes belonging to farmers who are taking water for their crops. After 0.33km you will find a turning to the right marked with a yellow arrow. For now follow the black pipes straight on until they disappear into one of several springs at the foot of a small cliff. These are the Melanhydros Springs referred to by Homer in *The Odyssey*. When the suitors were planning a feast, 20 maidservants went to draw water *'from the dark waters of the well'.* (20: 156) The huge cast of Homer's story wash and bathe at the Palace of Odysseus without any mention of water shortage and, when we look at the plentiful springs surrounding this site, we can be certain that it provided Odysseus, Penelope and their entire retinue with a good supply of fresh drinking water.

The Melanhydros Springs

The water that overflows in winter from the palace site finally disgorges into the harbour of Frikes. This harbour was called Rheithron in ancient times. Rheithron is the word for a 'watercourse' or 'torrent gulley' in Greek, and you will see an echo of that name in the word Platreithias, where this walk begins. During the winter rains the whole harbour at Frikes, and much of the road leading up from Frikes to Platreithias, can be flooded by torrents of water overflowing from this gulley. Frikes harbour was also, you will remember, the place where, in Homer's story, the goddess Athena moored her ship.

From the Melanhydros Springs return a short distance to the place where a yellow arrow indicates a right turn. Take this turn to the right and continue past a little old church that is said to be the site of an ancient temple.

The church to the left of the footpath

Then, after a set of modern steps, the path will cross a tarmac road. This is the new access road to the archaeological site. Were you to turn right along it you would reach the lower end of the site, however carry straight over the road and on up the ancient stepped path towards Exoghi. On your left you will pass a picnic shelter put up by the European Union and, after 0.54km from Gefuri restaurant, you will reach the upper gate into the archaeological site, which is currently not locked.

From here you can walk down through the site of the Palace of Odysseus as described in Chapter 14.

Welcome stranger to Kalamos Well,

Bend and drink from your cupped

hand its iced cold water

Breathe in around you the holy fragrance

And you shall return again to Ithaca.

Translation of a poem by E. Raftopoulos.

16

From the Palace of Odysseus to the Kalamos Spring and back to Platreithias

See map no.7, page 20

From the site of Odysseus' Palace to the freshwater spring at Kalamos. Distance 1.25km and 25 minutes to the spring plus another 1.2km and another 25 minutes to return to the Gefuri restaurant at Platreithias. Parts of this track are less clear, and less cleared, than the path up from Platreithias to the Palace of Odysseus but, following on from Walk No.15, this can make a good round trip following ancient paths and water sources.

Leaving the archaeological site of the Palace of Odysseus at Agios Athanasios by the lower gate, you will find yourself on the tarmac approach road. Turn to the left and continue northwards. This road is marked with the blue and white markers of the Trails of Greece mapping team and you will find it on their Avenza map.

Below the road, at a lower level, fenced areas surround unexcavated buildings from the Mycenaean era. One building is a very damaged, circular *kykloteres*, which is probably the base of a *tholos* or beehive tomb.

Here, a stone was found which appeared to represent Odysseus tied to the mast of his boat in order to resist the alluring songs of the Sirens. This object is yet to be displayed on Ithaca.

A clay tablet found at the kykloteres, possibly showing Odysseus and the Sirens

As you leave the palace site behind you the road becomes a dirt track. At 0.74km keep left, ignoring the track downhill to your right that goes to the hamlet of Kolieri. In the summer of 2021 a temporary fence had been erected across the road immediately before a place where, after about a kilometre and 15 minutes, you will find a footpath to your right. It is discreetly marked with a small wooden sign saying KALAMOS – (KOLIERI) EXOGI.

This ancient stepped donkey path has not been recently cleared. At 1.03km you pass a small house on the left. After 20 minutes at 1.07km you will reach a fence. The path turns sharp right here, so walk with the fence on your left. Dropping down to the left, the path is uncleared and narrow. After about 27 minutes at 1.24km you will reach the Kalamos Spring.

Kalamos Spring

I suggest you have a rest, fill up your water bottles and have a good drink, as this is the best spring water on the island. A sign reads:

Welcome stranger to Kalamos Well,
Bend and drink from your cupped hand its iced cold water
Breathe in around you the holy fragrance
And you shall return again to Ithaca.

Translation of a poem by E. Raftopoulos.

From the Kalamos Spring the walk back to the Gefuri restaurant at Platreithias is simply along the road. At 0.65km ignore the adjoining track from Kolieri to your right-hand side. At 0.83km you will find an interesting modern sculpture park on your left.

Sculpture Park

After 1.2km and about half an hour (or more if you spend time looking at the sculpture park) you will reach the Gefuri restaurant. With some luck, on a summer evening, you could find it open for a drink.

FROM THE PALACE OF ODYSSEUS

View of the ancient city of Alalkomenai

17

The Acropolis of Alalkomenai

See map no.8, page 21

The ascent to the acropolis of Alalkomenai is steep and you need to be reasonably fit to do it. The path is marked with red spots plus occasional red arrows. As long as you make no wrong turns it will take about 50 minutes to reach the summit. Distance 1.2km.

The site of the City of Alalkomenai at Aetos is impressive and well worth a visit. Archaeologists believe that this fortress was garrisoned in Mycenaean times but its main use came later, during the Dark Ages and that, at that time, the centre of habitation was on the saddle of land at the base of the hill.

There is a small car park just by the side of the road up from Piso Aetos, near a sign that points to the site, so leave your car or scooter here. You can join the path to the summit of Alalkomenai by first going to visit the small church of St. George. Then, when you come out of the door, turn right and you will see a rough pile of stones forming a step up from the area around the church. This will lead you towards the path to the summit. Alternatively you can go forward, bypassing the church on your right, and turn right near a water sterna, from where you can see the path clearly marked.

Turn left through some small ancient ruins with very steep stone steps.

Around this area, in 1931, Benton and Heurtley identified an ancient shrine, probably dedicated to Apollo. They dated it from around the time of Homer but well after the Mycenaean era of Odysseus. The obvious ruins you walk through are those of a later temple, from the 6th century BC, thus after the time of both Odysseus and Homer. It could have been built to replace the older structure.

Take the path upwards, following the red spots and arrows. Wrong turns will lead to ancient doorways and defensive walls.

When William Gell and Heinrich Schliemann visited Ithaca in the 19th century, the local people told them the summit of the conical hill of the City of Alalkomenai at Aetos was the site of the Palace of Odysseus, and this wrong identification has caused some ongoing confusion. A gap in local knowledge may have arisen when, during a brief and brutal Turkish rule in the 15th century AD, the islanders left Ithaca. The island was re-populated during the Venetian rule that followed.

The windy and inaccessible summit at Alalkomenai provides a perfect defensive position against attack, but it would not be a convenient place to live. It neither provides enough flat ground to accommodate the palace described by Homer nor fits his other descriptions of the Palace of Odysseus. There is no water source at the summit large enough to support an entire community, so extra water would have to be carried from the well at the base of the hill.

As you approach the summit you will pass a large water sterna. Red

circles will lead you to a well-defined path through the grass, heading north-west towards the concrete marker at the highest point, from where there are wonderful views.

The summit of Aetos was once suggested by the people of Vathi as the location of the Palace of Odysseus and it is often said that the early Homerist William Gell believed this was so. But, if you read the text of his book, you will find that he wasn't, actually, convinced of this at the time.

Archaeologists believe that the people of Ithaca retreated to this summit at times when the seas brought extreme danger. The site gives commanding views both westwards up and down the Ithaca Channel, and eastwards over the Gulf of Molos, where the entrances to the harbours of Dexia and Vathi can easily be seen. In the event of danger the people would have a choice of escape routes to two alternative seas, depending on the invaders' line of attack, but I think that the harbour at Polis Bay cannot be seen from here. Three rings of defensive walls surrounded the summit at Alalkomenai, and huge cut blocks still lie jumbled about.

Pay careful attention to the way you have come up so that you can locate your path for the return. Without mistakes the return should take 35 to 40 minutes.

Between 1984 and 1999, the archaeologist Sarantis Symeonoglou, from the Washington University of St Louis, excavated on this saddle of land below Alalkomenai / Aetos, near the small church of St George. He discovered, I am told, the remains of a Late Bronze Age building that could once have been a fountain. The artefacts there ranged from the Mycenaean period to the 4th century BC. The church itself was rebuilt after the earthquake in the 1950s but no ancient remains were found below it.

I understand that Symeonoglou believes the Palace of Odysseus once stood on the north-eastern slopes of Aetos. Like Heurtley and Benton he uncovered ruins there from the 9th century BC, a time following that of Odysseus but before the time of Homer. He claimed that the Palace of Odysseus once stood nearby but, as far as I am aware, he found no sign of it. However this is hearsay as Symeonoglou has yet to publish the results of his work on the 'Ithaca Project'.

A former Australian Classics graduate, international lawyer and diplomat Jonathan Brown has made a slightly different claim. In a beautifully produced and illustrated book *In Search of Homeric Ithaca*, published in 2020, he suggests that the palace of Odysseus once existed slightly higher on the slopes of Aetos, above the saddle of the hill but below the summit. To support his theory Brown picked the passage in Book 16 lines 341-353 where the words of Homer do not precisely fit the site at Agios Athanasios, see my explanation towards the end of Chapter 14, page 121. He also believed Agios Athanasios to be too far to walk from Eumaeus' Hut although, when Huxley checked this with two separate Ithacan shepherds, they both maintained the walk was feasible. Although his research was thorough, Brown unfortunately failed to locate the well-hidden paper written by Professor Thanasis Papadopoulos concerning his excavation at Agios Athanasios / School of Homer. He found no archaeological evidence to support his suggestion that the palace once existed at this site at Aetos and admitted that: "an archaeological dig on this site would probably be as futile as Schliemann's search for remains on the summit of Mount Aetos."

If anyone has archaeological evidence for an alternative position for the Palace of Odysseus on Ithaca that is more convincing than that presented by Litsa Kontorli-Papadopoulou and Thanasis Papadopoulos for the site at Agios Athanasios / School of Homer, let them put it forward. This is the only way that a proper assessment of these arguments can be made.

"My home is under the clear skies of Ithaca. Our landmark is Mount Neriton with its quivering leaves. Other islands are clustered round it, Dulichium and Same and wooded Zacynthus."

The Odyssey, Book 9: 21-24

Odysseus describes his home to King Alcinous.

18

Homeric Ithaca: Other Claims

In *The Odyssey* Homer tells how the clever and resourceful war hero Odysseus overcomes challenge after challenge before finally reaching his longed-for home island of Ithaca. It is known as a nostos poem, and the Greek word *nostos* is the root of our word nostalgia. It describes a longing for homecoming to a destination where, with all the experience gained from life, we return to our roots, and the hope is that unconditional love and acceptance will await us there. Homer's story of Odysseus' triumph over the countless perils faced on his long homeward journey is one that appeals to us all. His achievement is a fundamental desire of our human psyche.

Yet Homer's story has a darker side. Odysseus set out in twelve ships each manned by a full crew of men from his kingdom, but he returned alone. All his ships and all his men were lost. Also, in his long absence, 108 suitors, assuming that he was dead, began to woo his wife, Penelope. They hoped that one of them might take over his kingdom but, on his return, our hero Odysseus killed every one of them. The last pages of *The Odyssey* describe the predictable consequence when the families of the slaughtered suitors get together to seek their revenge. But finally, the goddess Athena steps in to establish peace and, against all the odds, Odysseus is saved again.

And will the hero of this tale live happily ever after? Unfortunately, after all these losses and killings, Odysseus cannot stay to enjoy a peaceful old age on his beloved island. In Book 11 of *The Odyssey* he is advised by the blind prophet Tiresias:

> *"But when you have killed these Suitors in your palace, by stratagem or in a straight fight with a naked sword, you must set out once more. Take a well-cut oar and go on till you reach a people who know nothing of the sea and never use salt with their food.... As for your own end, Death will come to you far away from the sea, a gentle Death."*

(11: 119-121 and 135-138)

An alternative ending was given in *The Telegony*, a sequel to *The Odyssey* written later by a different author. In this story Odysseus is mistakenly killed on Ithaca by Telegonus, a son conceived with the goddess Circe.

In spite of the likelihood that things will not end well, Odysseus' story of derring-do and homecoming still has enormous appeal; and this has had consequences. Many others, who are not Ithacan, want to adopt Odysseus for themselves. They imagine their own particular home as 'Ithaca' and, taking this line of thought further, they begin to believe that the true Greek island of Ithaca cannot, therefore, be the island described by Homer.

Even the most outlandish of these competing claims are passionately argued and backed up with quotations from ancient texts. It has been said, for instance, that Homeric Ithaca was actually, and variously, placed in Sicily, Spain, Denmark and in the Portuguese Azores in the mid-Atlantic Ocean! Claims that Odysseus' kingdom was centred in the larger and richer neighbouring islands of Corfu, Lefkas or Kefalonia are more believable, and some have achieved considerable, if dubious, success. In support of these arguments it has been suggested that the name Ithaca once belonged to a different island, or peninsula, due to a name change in medieval times. Yet this makes no sense. Coins found on Ithaca, and now in the Archaeological Museum in Vathi, in the British Museum, and elsewhere, show that Ithaca was called Ithaca as soon as coinage existed in the 4th and 3rd centuries BC. But, in spite of this, these arguments persist.

Although Homer's story specifically and repeatedly refers to Ithaca as an island where you arrive by boat, claims have recently been made that one or another peninsula of Kefalonia, to which the ancients could easily have walked on foot, are the real Homeric Ithaca. I will give three influential examples:

Makis Metaxas, Mayor of Poros of the Pronnoi district, claimed in his book published in 2000 that Homeric Ithaca was situated in his south-eastern region of Kefalonia. In 2005 the British management consultant Robert Bittlestone claimed in his book *Odysseus Unbound* that the north-western Paliki peninsula of Kefalonia was true Homeric Ithaca. In 2010 the Dutchman C H Goekoop, in his book *Where on Earth is Ithaca?* claimed that the north-eastern Erissos peninsula of Kefalonia, near the modern town of Fiscardo, was the true Homeric Ithaca. Kefalonia was, indeed, part of Odysseus' kingdom, but his kingdom was centred on Ithaca where Homer placed his longed-for home. There is no agreement between these three authors as to which area of Kefalonia was once called Ithaca and, in addition, there is no archaeological evidence matching Homer's descriptions of the palace to support any Kefalonian claim.

Bittlestone, with the help of Cambridge professor James Diggle and Edinburgh professor John Underhill, went to great lengths in an effort to prove his theory. He gave lectures at universities all over Europe and his theory generated newspaper stories all around the world. In the USA, the History Channel broadcast a programme, *Digging for Truth*, based on his hypothesis. Jon Snow described the new theory on a Channel 4 news broadcast, and a recording was immediately posted on a professionally made *Odysseus Unbound* website.

Bittlestone formed his theory about Paliki after reading an English translation of *The Odyssey* and studying satellite photographs of the area. He came to believe that the Paliki peninsula was once separated from the rest of Kefalonia by a sea strait making it a separate island. This, he surmised, would align better with the words of Homer. In an effort to prove his hypothetical channel existed at the time of Odysseus through to Homer, he entered into a research partnership with the international geoscience company Fugro, based in Holland. But, in spite of making 17 boreholes, helicopter-mounted electromagnetic and LiDAR surveys, ground-based resistivity and seismic refraction surveys, gravity surveys, and shallow marine seismic reflection surveys, Fugro was unable to support Bittlestone's claim. Meanwhile four Greek geologists, led by Professor Maroukian head of the Department of Geology at Athens University, also investigated Bittlestone's sea channel theory. They wrote a 63-page report in which they declared with certainty that Bittlestone's theory was not backed by geological fact, and concluded that if Paliki were ever separated from the rest of Kefalonia it was certainly not as late in geological time as the era of Odysseus through to Homer.

All the above authors, Metaxas, Bittlestone and C H Goekoop, claimed to base their hypotheses on Homeric texts; but these were carefully selected to support their particular argument. Texts that did not align with their theories were ignored. The analysis of Homeric texts is a complex subject and none of these authors were specialists. I have no specialist knowledge in this area either, but I was fortunate to have the help of the Classics professor, philologist and archaeologist George L Huxley to analyse the theoretical textual basis for these alternative claims.

In 2007, following a visit to one of Bittlestone's lectures, Huxley checked the ancient texts as they related to Ithaca. He followed the sea route taken by Telemachus on his homeward journey, which is carefully described by Homer, taking with him the most reliable Homeric texts in Ancient Greek and a copy of the periplus of pseudo-Skylax. This periplus, written in the 4th century BC, was an early attempt at a navigational chart. It describes the sea route around the Mediterranean working from one landmark to another. Huxley then revisited the traditional Homeric sites on Ithaca. I have described his views on the relevant texts and related matters in my book *Odysseus' Island*, so here I will simply summarise his main point.

Following the extensive research that Huxley suggested I realised that every single theory placing Homeric Ithaca anywhere other than the modern island of Ithaca is justified by the same two lines taken from *The Odyssey* Book 9. These form part of a speech where Odysseus describes his home island of Ithaca to the kindly king and queen of the Phaeacians. Huxley was not content to let me read this speech, and others, in an English translation. He told me that to properly understand the Homeric texts it is essential to go back to the best-authenticated version of the original Ancient Greek. He recommended Thomas W. Allen's edition of *The Odyssey* printed by the Oxford University Press in 1917, as a reliable text. In that edition the relevant lines of Odysseus' speech run as follows:

21 ναιετάω δ᾽ Ἰθάκην εὐδείελον· ἐν δ᾽ ὄρος αὐτῇ

22 Νήριτον εἰνοσίφυλλον, ἀριπρεπές· ἀμφὶ δὲ νῆσοι

23 πολλαὶ ναιετάουσι μάλα σχεδὸν ἀλλήλῃσι,

24 Δουλίχιόν τε Σάμη τε καὶ ὑλήεσσα Ζάκυνθος.

25 αὐτὴ δὲ χθαμαλὴ πανυπερτάτη εἰν ἁλὶ κεῖται

26 πρὸς ζόφον,

(9: 21-26 Homeri Opera, Tomus lll, second edition. Ed. Thomas W Allen. Oxford 1917. Reprinted 1965.)

This is difficult stuff, but it is necessary to explain Huxley's analysis. The classical philologist Thomas W. Allen did not publish an English translation of *The Odyssey*, but there is no disagreement on the meaning of the first part of this passage, lines 21-24. Here Odysseus explains that he comes from Ithaca, that it has a conspicuous landmark Mount Neriton, and that it is surrounded by other islands which he names as Doulichion, Same and Zacynthos. Huxley translates these four lines as follows:

I dwell in clearly-seen Ithaca. In it is a mountain with quivering foliage and conspicuous, Neriton. Around it there lie many islands very close to each other, Doulichion, Same, and wooded Zacynthos.

(9: 21-24 Huxley)

An alternative translation, made by E. V. Rieu in the Penguin Classics version of The Odyssey, is quoted at the head of this chapter. It is clear that Odysseus is referring to the same island of Ithaca that we know today, both because he calls it Ithaca and because Homer's description clearly fits the mountainous little island, surrounded by others (now called Lefkas, Kefalonia and Zacynthos) that we know today. The problem lies in the following lines 25-26. Huxley translates these two lines as follows:

'It, however, is low-lying and entirely uttermost in the sea towards the gloom.'

(9: 25-26 Huxley)

Although the original Greek doesn't say this, it is assumed in many English translations that the word 'it' (αὐτὴ at the beginning of line 25) also refers to Ithaca. If this were so, Huxley commented, the king and queen of Phaeacia, who were listening to Odysseus' speech, would have been very surprised! First, in lines 21-24, Odysseus says that Ithaca has a conspicuous mountain and is surrounded by other islands. Then, in lines 25-26, he says that 'it' is low-lying and furthest out to sea. Yet no island can be both 'mountainous and surrounded by others' and also 'low-lying and furthest out' in the sea. Although Huxley translates this passage as *entirely uttermost in the sea towards the gloom* many translations give it as *furthest out to sea to the west*. But this makes no odds as, however this passage is translated, no island can be both *surrounded by others* and *furthest out in the sea*, either to the west or in any other direction.

In Huxley's analysis there is a corruption in *The Odyssey* Book 9 lines 25-26 (in fact the omission of a single stroke of the stylus) and these lines do not refer to Ithaca at all. He believes they refer to the part of Odysseus' kingdom that is situated on mainland Greece. Yet, however this may be, it is still clear that no island, neither Ithaca nor anywhere else in the world, can fulfil the contradictory requirements of both lines 21-24 and lines 25-26. In addition, although lines 21-24 specifically state that Odysseus is referring to Ithaca in his description, and that description fits, this is not so for lines 25-26.

It is true that this philological problem has puzzled scholars since ancient times, but the idea that Homeric Ithaca might attach to a different island, or another place, is an idea that was given credence only in the early years of the 20th century, when Wilhelm Dörpfeld first proposed that Homeric Ithaca lay in Lefkas. In the context of circa 3,500 years that separate our time from that of Odysseus this doubt about the identity of Ithaca is a recent phenomenon. Until the end of the 19th century the occasional suggestions for alternative locations of Homeric Ithaca were not taken seriously, yet since then, and especially recently, they have picked up momentum. Some attract considerable funding and, no doubt, they also attract tourists.

In his book *In Search of Homeric Ithaca* Jonathan Brown has made a thorough study of these alternative hypotheses, both from Greece and elsewhere. He then gives lucid reasons to reject each one in turn and concludes "The story of *The Odyssey* matches the landscape of Ithaki to a striking degree" and "walking the landscape leaves me with a very strong impression that Homer must have known it personally". I agree with his verdict. The more I study the facts, the more I am certain that Ithaca is still Ithaca, as it has been from time immemorial. In my view the many and varied theories that Homeric Ithaca is a different place to the modern Greek island of Ithaca are quite simply wrong. I hope that, if you take the walks described in this book, you will arrive at the same conclusion.

Assuming that Homeric and modern Ithaca are one and the same, then where on Ithaca were the places described by Homer? In this guide, I have led you to the places most widely believed by scholars to be those described by Homer in *The Odyssey*, and this includes the Palace of Odysseus.

In the 1930s Heurtley and Benton from the British School at Athens made magnificent progress with their archaeological work on Ithaca, but when World War II interrupted their work, they hadn't yet reached agreement on the location of the Palace of Odysseus. Heurtley believed the palace would be found at Pelikata, to the north of the modern town of Stavros, while Benton believed it would be found at Agios Athanasios / School of Homer. (See Chapter 14.)

As I have explained in Chapter 17 there have been various claims that the palace would be found either on the summit, or on the saddle below Alalkomenai / Aetos, yet no archaeological evidence has been produced to support these claims.

The Greek archaeologists from the University of Ioannina, Professors Litsa

Kontorli-Papadopoulou and Thanasis Papadopoulos, were the first to find the foundations of a *megaron*, or main hall, from the age of Odysseus. Their work at Agios Athanasios has revealed the only Mycenaean palace structure as yet discovered and excavated on Ithaca (see Chapter 14). Not only this but, with the single exception that I have highlighted, their finds fit the words of Homer, as they said, 'like a glove'. Unfortunately Kontorli-Papadopoulou died suddenly without publishing a detailed record of her excavation at Agios Athanasios / School of Homer, but her husband and constant collaborator, the Professor of Archaeology Thanasis J Papadopoulos, gave some details of their work in a paper he gave at a conference at the Department of History and Archaeology in Ioannina in 2016. In his careful professional way he explained that this site "seems to be a promising and strong candidate for the political centre of the island and the Homeric Palace of Odysseus". In his view this location "most probably is that of the Palace of Odysseus". Up till now his paper has been very difficult to find but it can now be obtained more easily, see Recommended Reading at the head of Chapter 14.

Thanasis Papadopoulos and Litsa Kontorli-Papadopoulou are respected archaeologists, yet their conclusion that Agios Athanasios / School of Homer is the site of the Palace of Odysseus is still not officially accepted. Their discoveries fit the words of the poet Homer to an extraordinary degree, yet the location of the palace is still thought to be a matter of conjecture. This, taken together with the financial crisis of 2008, has led to a singular neglect of this important site. As I have explained in Chapter 14 the excavation pits are standing open and the site is currently both dangerous and vulnerable. There is no explanation on the site and more than 100 boxes containing finds from the excavation, including the Mycenaean bath discovered at the upper level and other finds from the time of Odysseus, have yet to be sorted, cleaned, recorded and displayed. In the meantime, with this guide, you too can look at the landscape and topography of Ithaca and make comparisons with the ancient words of Homer. By the time you have walked these walks I hope you will be as convinced as I am that the kingdom of Odysseus was centred on this island, and that Homeric and modern Ithaca are one and the same.

You may also be convinced that the Palace of Odysseus, as described by Homer, was situated in the Mycenaean site now known as Agios Athanasios / School of Homer. I believe this to be true, but these things can never be proved and some may disagree. One thing, however, I do know for sure. As an architect with a specialist conservation qualification I know that the Mycenaean remains at Agios Athanasios / School of Homer should not be left uncovered. This is a shocking state of affairs for any Mycenaean ruins, let alone ruins with a strong claim to be those of the Palace of Odysseus.

These ongoing arguments make the protection of this site problematic. Unlike the site of the battle of Troy, Agios Athanasios is not designated a World Heritage site. Greece has a wealth of magnificent ancient sites and, in this context, Agios Athanasios / School of Homer may not seem significant. However Homer's poem of *The Odyssey*, where he tells of Odysseus' return from the Trojan War, is literature of worldwide cultural importance. For this reason alone this known Mycenaean site on Ithaca should immediately be carefully protected and preserved.

A note about transliteration

Because the Greeks use their own alphabet the same name can appear in alternative forms when written in English. For instance, in the 21st century, the commonest spelling for Ithaca's larger neighbouring island is Kefalonia, but you can also find it spelled as Kefalinia, Cephallinia, Cephallenia, Cephalonia and in several other ways.

For the names of Ancient Greece, there is a convention that, because the Romans were the first people to write Greek names in our Roman alphabet, names are spelt as the Romans did. The word-endings are adapted to the structure of Latin. However Greek pronunciation has changed greatly over the millennia.

Although Modern Greek is, on the whole, spelled phonetically there is nowadays a choice between spelling modern names by replacing Greek letters with corresponding Roman letters or alternatively by reflecting their sounds. People do either, or mix different approaches. There is no ideal solution to this. I have tried to spell modern Greek names as they are commonly spelled but I cannot promise consistency. In quoting from others I have used the spellings used in the original.

Ithaca, Ithaka, Ithaki, Ithake or Thiáki are not different names. They are different transliterations of the Greek names Ἰθάκη or Θιάκη. The many ways of spelling Kefalonia are different transliterations of the Greek name Κεφαλλωνιά.

Essential information about Ithaca

The Greek island of Ithaca lies in the Ionian Sea to the east of the larger island of Kefalonia, from which it is separated by a 3-5km-wide strip of sea, the Ithaca Channel. Ithaca is about 24km long from top to toe, 8km wide at its widest point, and divided into two parts, the north and the south, joined mid-way by a narrow isthmus.

Accommodation
Accommodation is not always available on the island. It is advisable to book in advance, especially in peak season.

Ferries
The island has no airport, so unless you have a yacht or some other sea transport you will need to catch a ferry.

As of summer 2021 a large ferry, run by the Levante ferry company, sails from Patras on the mainland Peloponnese to Sami, and on to Piso Aetos (or Pisaetos) in Ithaca. In the winter months the timetable may be modified to suit passenger numbers or the ferry service may be cancelled. It is best to check this in the local office before you buy tickets. A smaller ferry, the Ionian Pelagos run by the Ionian P Lines, sails between Astakos on the mainland, Sami on Kefalonia, and Piso Aetos on Ithaca. Both these ferries arrive in Ithaca at Piso Aetos. This ferry port, which is quite a distance from any populated area, lies on the isthmus between the northern and southern parts of the island. The journey across the Ithaca Channel between Sami and Piso Aetos takes 30 to 40 minutes. Both in Sami on Kefalonia, and in Vathi on Ithaca, the big yellow Levante ferry is booked at a separate office to the Ionian Pelagos ferry. There is also a ticket booth on the quayside at Piso Aetos but, especially in high season or if you have a car, it is advisable not to rely on this.

In the summer months a small fair-weather ferry, which the locals call a 'slipper', runs between Frikes in north Ithaca and Nidri in Lefkas. Tickets can be bought in Nidri or at 'The Gods' tourist shop in Frikes.

I recommend that you check with the local port authority shortly before leaving that your ferry will run. This is especially important with the smaller ferries and in stormy weather.

Buses from Athens

Both the Ionian P and the Levante ferries connect with KTEL buses from Athens. You can book at the Athens bus station, KTEL Kifisou, right through to your destination. This is best, especially if you are catching the Levante ferry from Patras as, if you are carrying luggage, it is quite a walk from the bus station in Patras to the ferry port for Kefalonia and Ithaca.

For your return trip you will need to book tickets for the KTEL bus to Athens from Delas, the agent on the main square in Vathi. The buses come on board at Sami and you can put your cases onto the bus there.

Ithaca Port Authority

00 30 26743 60640. It is safest to check that the ferries are running if the weather blows up.

Piso Aetos

No bus meets the ferry at Piso Aetos and local taxis must be booked in advance. It is a 7km walk from Piso Aetos to Vathi so this is definitely advisable.

Taxis

For the north of the island Sue is English and very efficient: mobile 00 30 6944 289428 or sue@ithcatransfers.com and website www.ithacatransfers.com. Her husband, Dimos, also drives a taxi and they also have minibuses. For Vathi Spiros Grivas is good: 00 30 69708 51424 or spiros241@hotmail.com. The taxi rank in Vathi is adjacent to the main square on the opposite side of the road to the Ithaca Travel Tourist Office.

Tourist Agencies

There are now two private tourist agencies in Vathi.

Ithaca Tours in Vathi - 267403 3336; 69429 26660; info@ithacatours.gr

Ithaca Travel Tourist Office in Vathi – 26740 33267; info@ithacatravel.gr

The Ithaca Travel Tourist Office, on one side of the main square, will also arrange accommodation, guided walks and boat hire.

Medical

There are a hospital and two chemists in Vathi, and a chemist and a morning surgery in Stavros.

Police

Ithaca Police Station: 00 30 26740 32205. At the police station in Vathi there are a few policemen but you may find their English isn't perfect. On Ithaca the people are very self-sufficient. It is best for you to be self-sufficient too and, ideally, not to tangle with the police.

Car rental

This is possible from Alpha Cars in Vathi. Alternatively you can bring in a car from Kefalonia or elsewhere.

Petrol Stations

There are two petrol stations on the island, one in the south on the approach road into Vathi, and one in the north on the outskirts of Frikes.

Scooter and eBike rental

This is possible in Vathi.

Local Bus

There is only one bus between the north and the south of Ithaca. It is the school bus and it only runs in term time. It runs from Kioni, around through Frikes, Lachos, Platreithias and Stavros, to Vathi, and back by the same route. It leaves Kioni early in the morning (around 6.30am) and leaves Vathi around midday. Times vary and must be checked.

Boat Hire

There are various boat hire companies in Vathi. Their names are: Odyssey Outdoor Activities (tel: 00 30 69481 82655), Odyssey Sea Kayak, Odyssey Boats, Ithaca Boats or Rent-a-Boat Ithaca (tel: 00 30 69490 35670 or info@rentaboatithaca.com). My impression is that these companies cooperate with each other.

Acknowledgements

Most of all, on this project, I would like to thank my 'walk-checker' Nigel Summerley, who not only walked all the walks but carefully checked the text as well. I had totally underestimated the task of writing and checking this guide and I would have been quite stuck without his help. In addition he participated in invaluable interviews with two knowledgeable Ithacans, Spiros Couvaras and Andronikos Sakkatos. I would like to thank them too for generously sharing their time, knowledge and enthusiasm.

Help with research on the work at Agios Athanasios also came from the architect Dimitris Skirgiannis, who did the measurements and work on site for the lead archaeologist Litsa Kontorli-Papadopoulou and to her husband and fellow archaeologist, Thanasis J Papadopoulos, an expert in finds from the Mycenaean era.

For setting me on the right path with my studies and for help with the Ancient Greek texts I would again like to thank Professor George L Huxley for his help, generosity and extraordinary expertise.

Thank you to the architect and town planner Avghi Markopoulou for her help and advice on taking this work forward. Thank you to Nick Davies for his perceptive comments on the progress of the text. So many people have helped that I cannot hope to name them all.

I would like to thank all the wonderful people of Ithaca for their warm welcome to their beautiful island, especially Katerini Grigoriou for her enthusiasm and advice, and Dionisios Grivas for his reminder that all

Ithacans love their homeland and long to return. They are all remarkable individuals.

I wish I could thank those who have now left us. Firstly, of course, my dear husband Alec, who first brought me to this fascinating island way back in 1982 and shared it with me for over 30 years. And Denis Sikiotis who was the first to organise the clearing and marking of the ancient footpaths that he remembered as a boy.

Finally a huge thank you to Tabby Bourdier of Loco Design for her interest, expertise and endless care and patience with the typesetting and graphic design of the text and cover, and to Steve Foot for his help and, of course, his ePub knowhow.

Selected bibliography

BENTON S. Excavations in Ithaca lll. The Cave at Polis l. British School at Athens.

BENTON S. Excavations at Stavros, Ithaca. British School at Athens 47. 1937

BENTON S. British School at Athens 68 (1973) Excavations on Ithaca at Tries Lagades.

BITTLESTONE R. with DIGGLE J. and UNDERHILL J. Odysseus Unbound, The Search for Homer's Ithaca. Cambridge University Press 2005.

BROWN J. In Search of Homeric Ithaca. Parrot Press, Canberra 2020.

DE GRUYTER W. Kadmos. Zeitschrift für vor und frühgriechische Epigraphik. Walter de Gruyter 2005.

GELL W. The Geography and Antiquities of Ithaca – Primary Source Edition. 1807.

GOEKOOP C. Where on Earth is Ithaca? Eburon Academic Publishers, Delft. 2010.

HEURTLEY W. Excavations in Ithaca ll The Early Helladic Settlement at Pelikata. British School at Athens 35 (1935) pp.45-73.

HOPE SIMPSON and LAZENBY. The Catalogue of Ships in Homer's Iliad. Oxford 1970.

HUXLEY G. Ulixes Redux: Why the Island called Ithaki today is Homer's Ithaca. Unpublished lecture notes. Professor George Huxley for the Friends of the British School at Athens on 7th November 2007.

HUXLEY G. Review of Odysseus Unbound: The Search for Homer's Ithaca by Robert Bittlestone, James Diggle and John Underhill. Hermathena 2007.

KONTORLI-PAPADOPOULOU L. and PAPADOPOULOS T. Proceedings of the VIIIth conference (2 - 7 September 2000) on The Odyssey. Issued by the Centre for Odyssey Studies, and collected in a volume titled Eranos.

KONTORLI-PAPADOPOULOU L. PAPADOPOULOS T. and OWENS G. A Possible Linear Sign from Ithaki (AB09 'SE')

KONTORLI-PAPADOPOULOU and KNAUSS J. The Prehistoric underground well-house at Ithaka at the so-called School of Homer. Kontorli-Papadopoulou L. Eranos and Corpus 2001.

KONTORLI-PAPADOPOULOU L. Corpus 28. Αρχαιολογια Ιστορια των Πολιτισμων Ζεύγμα. ΙΘΑΚΗ 2011.

LUCE J.V. Homer and the Heroic Age. Harper Collins 1975.

LUCE J.V. Celebrating Homer's Landscapes. Troy and Ithaca Revisited, Yale University Press 1988.

LUCE J. The Identity of Ithaca: Decisive New Geological Information about the Thynia Isthmus in Kefalonia. The Classical Association News No.37 December 2007.

MALKIN I. The Returns of Odysseus: Colonization and Ethnicity. University of California Press 1998.

PAIZIS-DANIAS D. Homer's Ithaca on Cephallenia? Facts and Fancies in the History of an Idea. Ithaca Friends of Homer Association.

PAIZIS-DANIAS D. Throwing Light on Homeric Ithaca. Exhibition at Stavros Ithaca 2013 onwards.

PAIZIS-DANIAS D. The Archaeological Treasures of Ithaca.

PAPADOPOULOS Th. J. Mycenaean citadels of Western Greece: Architecture, purpose and their intricate role in the local communities and their relations with the West. Published in Aegaeum 41: The Aegean Seen from the West. Proceedings of the 16th International Aegean Conference, University of Ioannina, Department of History and Archaeology, Unit of Archaeology and Art History, 18–21 May 2016. Page 419 onwards.

PAPADOPOULOS Th. J. The Heroon of Odysseus at Ithaca. Reconsidered. University of Ioannina online 2022.

RIEU D.C.H. The Iliad and The Odyssey. Penguin Classics Revised Translation 1991.

SCHLIEMANN H. Ithaka, der Peloponnes und Troja. 1869. Facsimile Publisher 2013.

SOUYOUDZOGLOU-HAYWOOD C. The Ionian Islands in the Early Bronze Age 3000-800. Liverpool University Press 1999.

SOUYOUDZOGLOU-HAYWOOD C. Archaeology and the Search for Homeric Ithaca. The Case of Mycenaean Kephalonia. ACTA Archaeologica Vol.89. Wiley 2018.

STANFORD and LUCE. The Quest for Ulysses. Phaidon 1974.

TALBOT R.A. Ed. Barrington Atlas of the Greek and Roman World. Princeton 2000.

TSAKOS C.I. Ithaca and Homer (The Truth). Athens 2005. Translated into English by Geoffrey Cox.

WACE and STUBBINGS. A Companion to Homer. Macmillan 1962.

WATERHOUSE H. British School at Athens 91 (1996) pp.301-317. From Ithaca to the Odyssey.

WOOD M. In Search of the Trojan War. BBC Books 1985.

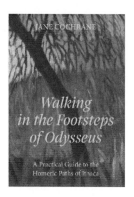

If you have any feedback or comments about the state of the footpaths I describe, please could you write me a note to info@janeocochrane.co.uk? Then I will do my best to check and update my information.

If you have enjoyed reading this guide, or have found it useful, please consider leaving a review on Amazon UK, Amazon US or on my website:

www.janeocochrane.co.uk

Even a line or two would be very helpful.

REVIEWS

Thoroughly praiseworthy

In *Odysseus' Island* Jane Cochrane showed that the Ithaca of Homer is the island called Ithaca today. Her second contribution to Ithacan studies: *Walking in the Footsteps of Odysseus: A Practical Guide to the Homeric Paths of Ithaca* adds to arguments for the identification by explaining the internal geography of the isle, with particular attention to journeys on foot made by Odysseus, Telemachus, and Eumaeus. The well-shod visitor is thus enabled to walk the Homeric pathways. The book is a delightful combination of literary investigation with severe practicality – Cochrane knows that it is possible to become lost even in a small island and tells the reader what to do if a wrong turning has been taken. She and her 'walk-checker' provide times and distances tested by traversing Ithaca's varying terrain and there is prudent guidance on such topics as ferries and car rental. The need to use accurate maps – some are seriously misleading – is emphasized. Her own are well tied to the narrative. The description of the palatial remains at Agios Athanasios, neglected and unpublished as they are, will be especially welcome to devotees of Homer. Her systematic and instructive book is thoroughly praiseworthy.

Professor George L Huxley

Obviously a labour of love by the writer, this very well written book sets out the trails in detail with a dollop of Homer quotes to keep the walker entertained and enthralled. I cannot wait to strap my walking boots on.

Alison Jane Macro

The walks follow the narrative of Odysseus's arrival on Ithaca and end with an exploration of his palace, where he took care of his wife's 108 suitors. They have all been tested and timed and there is a wealth of detail on the paths to follow. Each walk is illustrated by relevant quotations from the Odyssey as well as photos of the views to expect and the walk to the site of the palace is illustrated and discussed in detail. Then there is an informed discussion of whether Ithaca is the true home of Ulysses, and an assessment of the significance of the other archaeological sites on the island. Finally, there are tips on getting there and getting around - ferries, boat and car hire, taxis etc. In short, this is a really useful book. The best walking books don't just tell you where to go but give a sense of the places, a meaning. This book is in this tradition. I read it with growing admiration for the author's energy and erudition.

George Paizis

This book holds three conversations with the reader: the question of modern Ithaca (Ithaki) is Homer's Ithaca (Ithake), the locations on Ithaca and how far they correspond or not with the sites described in the Odyssey, and finally the walks (or in some cases hikes) themselves. Jane Cochrane has discussed some of the issues with locating Homer's Ithaca and with the sites on modern Ithaca in her earlier book Odysseus' Island. In this book she sums up the arguments. She shows very clearly that the arguments against modern Ithaca as Homer's Ithaca (an idea that started with Wilhelm Dörpfeld claiming that a part of modern Lefkas was Homer's Ithaca) are basically worth nil. She also very persuasively argues that some of the locations on Ithaca must be the ones mentioned in the Odyssey. And then when we come to the descriptions of the walks along the paths of

Ithaca, they are excellent. For the last eight years my wife and I have been walking and hiking over most of Ithaca - and have lost our ways a few times as Cochrane warns in her book. I find her guide to the walks on Ithaca the best I have read. I highly recommend this book.

Espen Smith Ore

Made in United States
North Haven, CT
19 February 2023

32872525R00093